THE PRINCETON REVIEW

Cracking the SAT II: ENGLISH Subject Tests

THE PRINCETON REVIEW

Cracking the SAT II: ENGLISH Subject Tests

LIZ BUFFA AND ADAM ROBINSON

1998-99 EDITION

RANDOM HOUSE, INC.
NEW YORK 1998

Princeton Review Publishing, L.L.C.
2315 Broadway
New York, NY 10024
E-mail: info@review.com

ISSN: 1076-5395
ISBN: 0-375-75099-1

SAT II is a registered trademark of the College Board.

Edited by: Amy Bryant
Designed by: Illeny Maaza
Production Editor: Scott Falk

Manufactured in the United States of America on partially recycled paper.

9 8 7 6 5 4 3 2 1

ACKNOWLEDGMENTS

I would like to thank the following people for their invaluable assistance: Dominick Buffa, Marcia Lerner, Illenly Maaza, Cynthia Brantley, Alicia Ernst, Amy Bryant, Scott Falk, my students, and my parents, David and Mary Anne Bradley.

A special thanks to Yung-Yee Wu and B. Young for their expertise in the art of writing diags.

CONTENTS

PART I

Overview

1

The Route to College

If you've purchased this book, you are probably on the road that will ultimately lead to college. With some luck and a little know-how, combined with your accomplishments to date, it will be a road to the college of your choice.

Part of this long and arduous admissions process will almost certainly include some standardized tests. For most of you, these tests will come from Educational Testing Service (ETS). (We'll talk more about ETS in a little while.) The most familiar of these tests is the Scholastic Assessment Test, or SAT I.

What Is the SAT I?

The SAT I is not a measure of your intelligence. It is only a measure of your ability to take a standardized test.

The SAT I is a three-hour, multiple-choice exam used by colleges to provide a standard measure of high school students around the country. There are two separate scores generated by the SAT I: a verbal score (on a scale of 200–800), and a math score (again, on the 200–800 scale).

What Does the SAT Measure?

Precious little. Some vocabulary, some reading skill, some basic math (sixth- through ninth-grade level). Primarily, it measures your ability to take standardized tests. What it's designed to measure is your ability to perform in college. What it's better at measuring is your gender, race, and family income level. What it's very bad at measuring is your intelligence.

What Are the SAT II: Subject Tests?

These are a series of one-hour exams administered by the Educational Testing Service.

Unlike the SAT I, the SAT II: Subject Tests are designed to measure specific knowledge in specific areas. There are many different tests in many different subject areas such as biology, history, French, and math. They are scored separately on the familiar 200–800 scale.

How Are SAT II: Subject Tests Used by College Admissions?

Since the tests are given in specific areas, colleges use them as another piece of admissions information and, often, to decide if an applicant can be exempted from college requirements. For example, a certain score may excuse you from a basic English class or a foreign language requirement.

Should I Take the SAT II: Subject Tests? How Many? When?

You should take SAT II: Subject Tests only if the schools to which you are applying require them.

About one-third of the colleges that require SAT I scores also require that you take two or three SAT II: Subject Tests. Your first order of business is to start reading those college catalogs. College guidebooks, admissions offices, and guidance counselors should have this information as well.

As to which tests you should take, the answer is simple:

1. those Subject Tests that you will do well on, and
2. the tests that the colleges you are applying to may require you to take.

The best possible situation, of course, is when the two match.

Some colleges have specific requirements, others do not. Again, start asking questions before you start taking tests. Once you find out what the required tests are, if there are any, part of your decision making is done. The next step is to find out which of the tests will show your particular strengths. Colleges that require specific tests generally suggest the following three:

- Writing Test
- Math Level IC or Level IIC
- something else

Choosing the "something else" means having to evaluate your own strengths and skills. Possibilities range from English literature, American or European history, biology, chemistry, and physics, to a variety of foreign languages.

As for when, take the tests as close as possible to the corresponding coursework you may be doing. If you plan to take the SAT II: Chemistry Test, for example, and you are currently taking chemistry in high school, don't postpone the test until next year.

Typically, schools that require Subject Tests ask you to take the Writing Test, either the Math IC or IIC Test, and a third test of your choice.

WHEN ARE THE SAT II: SUBJECT TESTS OFFERED?

In general, you can take from one to three Subject Tests in up to three separate subject areas in October, November, December, January, May, and June at test sites across the country. All subjects are offered at each administration.

There are two distinct Subject Tests offered in the field of English. They are:

- the Writing Test—this test has multiple-choice questions and a 20-minute essay. The questions focus primarily on grammar and sentence structure.

- the English Literature Test—this has only multiple-choice questions focusing on content.

There are two Subject Tests in the field of English: the Writing Test and the English Literature Test.

HOW DO I REGISTER FOR STANDARDIZED TESTS?

Pick up a registration form and *Student Bulletin* at your guidance office. You may also write to or call the College Board at:

College Board ATP
P.O. Box 6200
Princeton, New Jersey 08541-6200
(609) 771-7600 (Monday–Friday 8:30 A.M.–9:30 P.M. EST)

The fee you pay to register will enable you to take the aforementioned one to three separate tests. That means you can take a single one-hour test and leave, or take two or three different one-hour tests. If you are taking the Writing Test, though, it must be the first test you take. It's only administered during the first hour of testing. You may have the scores sent to you, to your school, and to four colleges of your choice. Additional reports will be sent to additional colleges for, you guessed it, additional money. The scores take about six weeks to arrive. You'll also have the option of looking at your scores first and deciding which will go on to your colleges—for a fee, of course! You can also order the Writing Sample Copy Service and get three copies of your scored essay to include with your applications, if you're so inclined.

What Is Score Choice?

Score Choice is a special option offered for Subject Tests only. With Score Choice, you can see your scores *before* they are sent to schools. You can also choose which scores you want released to schools.

This is a new service for those of you taking the SAT II: Subject Tests. If you're not in a rush to get your scores to your colleges, you may elect at the time you register for the test to use Score Choice. Score Choice allows you to see your scores before they are sent to your colleges, and decide which of them you want released to the schools.

It's probably a good idea to use Score Choice anytime you're not in a hurry. This way you'll never have to send a bad score out with your application. Are there any drawbacks? Well, normally, you would get your scores sent to four colleges with the price of registration. Although Score Choice itself costs nothing, you no longer get those free schools. When you're ready to release your scores, you send off a release form, with a payment for each transcript sent to each college.

Do not misuse Score Choice, however, and overdo all the test taking because only the best ones will be seen by your college. It's still not a good idea to take any SAT-type test more than a few times. You will burn out. You also may want to take fewer than the three tests at one sitting. See what your stamina is. If three is too many, just take one or two at a time.

What's a Good Score?

Please note (especially if you are a senior) that using Score Choice can cause a delay in the reporting of your scores to schools.

That's hard to say, exactly. A good score is a score that fits in the range of scores the college of your choice usually accepts or looks for. However, if your score falls below the normal score range for Podunk University, that doesn't mean you won't go to Podunk University. Schools are usually pretty flexible in what they are willing to look at as a "good" score for a certain student.

You'll receive with your score a subscore for the writing sample and the multiple-choice part of the test (for the Writing Test) and a percentile rank. That number tells you how you fit in with the other test takers. In other words, a percentile rank of 60 means that 40 percent of the test takers scored above you and 60 percent scored below you.

What Is The Princeton Review?

The Princeton Review is a test-preparation company based in New York City. We have branches in more than fifty cities across the country and abroad. We've developed the techniques you'll find in our books and courses by analyzing actual exams and testing their effectiveness with our students. What makes our techniques unique is our approach. We base our principles on the same ones used by those people who write the test. We also don't want to waste your time with superfluous information. We're not going to teach you "English Grammar in Fifty Easy Steps" or "How to Appreciate Fine English Literature," but rather, just the information you'll need to get great score improvements. You'll learn to recognize and comprehend the relatively small amount of information that's actually tested. You'll also learn to avoid common traps, to think like the test writers, to find answers to questions you're unsure of, and to budget your time effectively.

We don't waste your time: We tell you what you need to know and, more important, what you *don't* need to know.

You need to do only two things: trust the techniques, and practice, practice, practice.

Is There Any Other Material Available for Practice?

Stay away from the plethora of test-prep books available. The questions in the majority of books on the market bear little, if any, resemblance to actual SAT II: Subject Test questions. As the SAT II: Subject Tests are new, following in the footsteps of the Achievement Tests, you may have trouble finding actual full-length tests on which to practice. *The Official Guide to the SAT II: Subject Tests,* although a rewrite of old Achievement Tests, is now available and contains full-length tests. "Taking the SAT II: Subject Tests," a booklet published by The College Board, will also have sample questions.

After you've completed all the practice tests and drills in this book, prove to yourself that the techniques we've outlined work on actual tests.

2

Approaching the SAT II: English Subject Tests

THE SAT II: ENGLISH TESTS — THE SPECIFICS

The Writing Test lasts for one hour. It consists of one essay question (20 minutes) followed by 60 multiple-choice questions (40 minutes).

As we mentioned before, there are two distinct SAT II Tests offered in English. One is the Writing Test, the other is the Literature Test.

The Writing Test, as the name implies, covers basic writing and grammar skills. Can you put a sentence together? Can you rewrite a paragraph? And can you write a basic essay? The Writing Test begins with a 20-minute writing exercise, which will give you a chance to show ETS your writing prowess by writing a simple essay. The essay section is followed by a 40-minute multiple-choice section, which gives you a chance to show ETS your filling-in-the-bubble prowess by answering questions about how sentences and paragraphs should be written. As noted before, colleges that require three specific tests often want you to take the Writing Test.

The Literature Test also lasts for one hour. It consists of 60 multiple-choice questions.

The English Literature Test will test your knowledge of very basic literary terms and your ability to understand and analyze selected literary passages. You'll have an hour to answer sixty multiple-choice questions. You'll need to be able to interpret the material based on a general knowledge of literature, but the test won't cover specific books, authors, or periods. The English Literature Test is usually not required by colleges that request specific tests, but some schools might use a higher score on it to exempt you from basic English courses. If you feel confident about your abilities in English Literature, consider taking the SAT II in that subject.

PART ◆ II

The SAT II:
Writing Test

3

Cracking the Writing Test

What Is This Writing Test Supposed to Test?

As the name implies, the SAT II: Writing Test is purported to assess some writing ability. If a multiple-choice test of writing ability seems like an oxymoron to you, congratulations! You have just passed "Discerning Test Taking 101." The good news for you is that this format makes it quite easy to learn what ETS considers to be a valid indicator of writing ability in short order.

If this leads you to exclaim, "But what about that essay?" consider this: Since graders have about two minutes to read your essay, they won't be considering things like originality when evaluating it. It's really no more difficult to figure out what you need to do to write an acceptable essay than it is to figure out how to get the right answer on a multiple-choice question.

Even though the Writing Test claims to assess your writing ability, the majority of questions are multiple choice.

How Is the Writing Test Structured?

The test begins with a 20-minute writing sample. It also has approximately sixty questions in three different sections. You get 40 minutes to finish the multiple-choice section, which is structured like this:

- Identifying Sentence Errors—30 questions
- Improving Sentences—18 questions
- Improving Paragraphs—12 questions

The multiple-choice section of the Writing Test is made up of three question types: Identifying Sentence Errors, Improving Sentences, and Improving Paragraphs.

Now that you've gotten a general feeling for the structure of the test, let's go over some basic principles you should adopt right away. Some of these ideas may run contrary to the notions you've had for years about test taking. Remember one thing—our goal is to get you a good score, not to impress your high school English teacher.

How the SAT II: Writing Test Is Like the SAT I

Scoring

For those of you who may not be familiar with the standard ETS method of scoring exams, here's a quick review.

If you get a question right————you get 1 point

If you get a question wrong————you lose $\frac{1}{4}$ point

If you leave a question blank————nada, nothing

For every question you get right, you receive 1 point; for every question you get wrong, you lose $\frac{1}{4}$ point.

Let's pretend that you had a really bad night the night before the exam. No sooner do you sharpen your pencil than you fall asleep, waking only to hear the proctor call that you have five minutes. In a frenzy, you simply decide to mark random guesses on every question.

In a statistically perfect world, since there are five answer choices for each question, you would get one out of every five random responses right—following so far? ETS has accomplished its primary goal: to eliminate the possibility that you will pick up points randomly guessing.

One right = +1 point; four wrong = $-\frac{1}{4} \times 4 = -1$ point

Now, let's imagine the same scenario, only this time your friend, who notices that you are snoring, nudges you awake with just ten minutes to spare. You can't possibly read all the questions and all the choices, so you simply eliminate one obviously wrong choice from each set of answers and *then* guess.

You just picked up points.

In our statistically perfect world, since you were now choosing from just four possibilities instead of five, you would get one of every four questions right (+1 point) and three wrong ($-\frac{3}{4}$ point). By the end, you've gained a few points at least.

All of this leads to our BIG IMPORTANT RULE (so big and important that you will read it many times before you've finished this book):

> ANYTIME YOU CAN ELIMINATE EVEN
> ONE WRONG ANSWER, YOU MUST GUESS.

As we will demonstrate, it's pretty easy to eliminate wrong answers on the Writing Test, so you should be leaving *very few* blanks.

If you can eliminate just one wrong answer, guess.

Pacing

This chart is important. It demonstrates that it's not necessary to answer every question to get a really super score. Figure out how many you can just let go.

You can leave	get	and still get
38 blank	7 wrong	500
25 blank	5 wrong	600
10 blank	3 wrong	700

You don't have to answer every question in order to get a good score—so *slow down*. Accuracy is more important than speed.

So stop rushing! You'll be just fine.

Don't ever hesitate to skip a few as you go. It's not a bad idea to finish off all the questions that immediately hit you before tackling the ones that will take some thought. By the time you've finished all the practice drills, you will certainly read some questions and know immediately what's wrong with them. Do as many of those as you can first.

Why not just do everything in the order in which it is presented? There are a couple of reasons for this. First of all, you want to feel good about things as soon as you sit down. Being defeated by a question at the beginning may cause you to lose heart. You may simply need to warm up a little. Since forty minutes is not a long time, you don't want to warm up halfway through the multiple-choice section. Jumping around and finishing the easy questions first will make you feel better and will warm you up for the more difficult questions.

The second reason you should jump around is that you don't want to waste any time. That means first polishing off the questions that take the least amount of time.

Doing the easiest, fastest questions first ensures more time for the harder, more time-consuming questions, and also, if you run out of time, it will be where you least need it—on the questions you might have gotten wrong anyway.

Before you start, remember the words on the cover of *The Hitchhiker's Guide to the Galaxy*:

DON'T PANIC.

Order of Difficulty

ETS claims that the questions at the beginning of each section are easier than the questions at the end of each section. This is not really true. Don't panic if one of the first questions you read is impossible. Skip it. Or eliminate a choice or two and make a guess.

By the same token, don't second guess yourself if one of the last questions in a section seems to have a really obvious answer. It's probably just what you think it is.

HOW DO I KNOW IF I SHOULD TAKE THE WRITING TEST?

Sign up for the Writing Test if:

1. the colleges of your choice require it (some ask specifically for the Writing Test)

2. you feel comfortable with your writing and basic grammar skills

If you're still on the fence about this, take some of the diagnostic drills in this book and see if the Writing Test is best for you.

HOW TO USE THIS BOOK

The book is structured to give you a grammar overview first. There are drills and tips for each type of grammar rule or potential error that comes up on the test. We go through this section first.

There is no need to get bogged down with lots of ridiculous terms like "predicate nominative" or "present perfect progressive tense" because *you don't need to know these things to get a great score*. At no point are you tested on the names of all these grammar things. All you need to learn is how to recognize what's right and what's wrong. The few terms used are just there to explain concepts.

After you've mastered the nuances of grammar, move on to discussions about each question type: how to approach it, how to get more points. We'll show you how your knowledge of the grammar we've discussed combined with techniques we'll explain can help you get a better score on the Writing Test.

4

Grammar, Grammar, Grammar

If you sat down today to read through the rules of grammar in preparation for the Writing Test, you would find a wide variety of books on the subject. They would examine every nuance and rule and you would be cross-eyed before you were finished. Luckily for you, this isn't necessary. The Writing Test actually tests a remarkably small number of grammatical rules. ETS knows just the kind of mistakes you tend to make—the kind of things you might not notice in a written sentence—and tests these concepts over and over and over.

DEFINITION OF TERMS

Before we dive into the grammar part, let's take a minute to define some basic terms. Again, you will *not* be tested on any of these definitions on the test, but for the purposes of our review it will be imperative to know the difference between a noun and a pronoun.

ETS is very predictable: It likes to test the *same* grammatical rules from year to year.

Noun—a person, place, or thing
This *book* is handy.

Pronoun—a word that takes the place of a noun
Because *it* is so small, this book is handy.

Verb—an action word. Verbs may also express a state of being.
I *find* this book handy.
This book *is* handy.

Adjective—a word that describes a noun
This book is *handy*.

Adverb—a word that describes a verb, an adjective, or another adverb
This book is *so very* handy.

Phrase—a group of words that cannot stand alone as a sentence because it lacks either a subject or a verb. It is a *phrase*, though, because the words work together in a sentence as a noun, a verb, an adverb, or an adjective.
This book, *by the way*, is so very handy.

Preposition—a word that shows the relationship of a noun or pronoun to something. Words like *in, out, at, into, behind, to, from*, and *around* are prepositions. A preposition is found in a . . .

Prepositional phrase—a phrase that begins with a preposition
This book, *with the red cover*, is so handy.

Clause—a group of words, which, unlike a phrase, has a subject and a verb. Like a phrase, it is a group because the words work together in the sentence. Some clauses can stand alone, without the rest of the sentence, while others need the rest of the sentence to make sense.
Because it is so small, *this book is handy.*

Because it is so small is the first clause. It cannot stand alone—it wouldn't make much sense without the rest of the sentence. What it does is describe *why* the book is handy, and as such it acts as an adverb.

The second part of the sentence, *this book is handy*, is also a clause. It's the *main clause*, because it can stand alone.

ALL YOU'LL EVER NEED TO KNOW

As we've mentioned, precious little is actually tested on the SAT II: Writing Test. With a little practice you can train yourself to notice what you're being tested on and to immediately check the possible answer choices. Let's start by illustrating the five most common errors on the test. If these sentences sound perfect to you, you're just the kind of test taker ETS hopes for. These are common mistakes that everybody makes. If you notice the mistake, circle it: You'll be that far ahead of the game before we even start.

Don't worry, an explanation about each error follows. We'll go into each error type in depth and drill you later in the chapter.

To crack the Writing Test, focus on the five most common error types.

THE FIVE MOST COMMON ERRORS TESTED

Each of these sentences demonstrates a commonly tested error. See if you can spot it. If not, the answers immediately follow.

1. Last year, I'm going crazy from standardized tests.

2. Neither of us want to go to that movie.

3. Whenever you bring a friend to visit, make sure they bring their bathing suit.

4. Between you and I, this is the greatest book I've ever read.

5. I was concerned with what my guidance counselor told me.

It's a good time to notice that even though we're going to be tossing around some grammatical terms, it's not necessary to understand why a sentence is wrong when you take the test. There are no questions that say "What type of error is this?" You need only become adept at recognizing errors and pointing them out.

Let's go over what we just did.

1. The sentence should read:
   Last year, I *went* crazy from standardized tests.

Explanation:

This is a problem of **tense**. Although you don't need to keep the tense in a sentence the same all the way through, it does need to make sense. You could say, for example:

Are the verbs in the right tense?

"Last year, after taking my test, I was despondent; this year, after preparing for the test, I am ecstatic."

Decide what the author means. It's impossible to "go crazy" (present tense) "last year." Last year is in the past and you must use the past tense to express something you did *then*.

2. The sentence should read:
   Neither of us *wants* to go to that movie.

Explanation:

Do the subject and verb agree?

This is a problem of **subject-verb agreement.** Here, the subject "neither" is singular. You have to use a singular verb to go with it. The most common mistakes arise around those wacky, ambiguous pronouns like "neither," "either," "none," "everybody," "everyone," and so on. These words often sound like they are referring to more than one person, but technically, they're not. For example, everybody means "every single body." Check that the verb matches its subject in form.

3. The sentence should read:
   Whenever you bring a friend to visit, make sure *he* brings *his* bathing suit.

Explanation:

Does the pronoun agree with the noun it replaces?

This is a problem of **pronoun agreement**. Whenever you replace a noun with a pronoun, it must use the same form as the noun it replaces. Here, the pronoun "he" refers to "a friend." It's a common mistake when replacing singular nouns with singular pronouns to use "they." The reason? "He/she" sounds ridiculous, we can all agree. "One" sounds stuffy. And who, in these politically correct times, wants to commit to either a "he" or a "she"? So what happens? You say "they." It sounds better, but it's wrong.

4. The sentence should read:
   Between you and *me*, this is the greatest book I've ever read.

Explanation:

Is the case of the pronoun correct?

This is a problem of **pronoun case.** In other words, when do you say "I" and when do you say "me"? When do you say "who" and when do you say "whom"? Here again there are some common mistakes that are easily recognized once you get in the habit of noticing them.

5. The sentence should read:
   I was concerned *about* what my guidance counselor told me.

Explanation:

Does the idiom use the right words?

This is a problem of **idiom.** This is definitely the weird one in the bunch. Idiom is quite simply the way we put words together. The best you can do is go over a list of common idioms, and be aware that the strange-sounding prepositions may be just that—strange. You'll become more adept at spotting these after a few drills.

SOME MORE COMMON MISTAKES

Now that we've identified the most common mistakes on the test, try your hand at some of the rest of the typical mistakes found. Again, don't worry if these sound good—they're *meant* to.

6. Susan likes to play piano, to read good books, and ~~buying~~ *to buy* nice clothes.

7. David and Paul are looking for a girlfriend.

8. Evita won't be going out tonight and she's grounded.

9. The kids at our school are much smarter than the other school.

10. After seeing the new movie, Daniel Day-Lewis was the group's favorite new star.

11. The news stories were incredulous.

12. The meeting is scheduled for 4:00 P.M. this afternoon.

13. That is to say, the way you asked for it.

14. I <u>don</u>'t have <u>scarcely</u> any money to spend.

15. Of the fifteen people at the party, Marielle is the more beautiful.

16. She was running so quick that I couldn't catch her.

17. Dominick told Henry that he couldn't finish the job.

Not so easy? Let's look at the answers. Remember, the names of the errors are not important. You'll be asked to identify or correct an error, not to name one.

6. The sentence should read:
   Susan likes to play piano, to read good books, and *to buy* nice clothes.

Explanation:

The problem here is **parallelism**. Whenever you list actions, they must be in the same form (here, **to** play, **to** read, and **to** buy).

> Are the items in the list parallel?

7. The sentence should read:
   David and Paul are looking for *girlfriends*.

Explanation:

This is a problem of **noun agreement.** You've got two people as subjects out there looking, so logically, you must have two things they are looking for. Unless, of course, they are looking for one girlfriend to share.

> Does the noun agree with the noun to which it refers?

8. The sentence should read:
   Evita won't be going out tonight *because* she's grounded.

Explanation:

Here, the wrong **conjunction** was used. Conjunctions are used to bring parts of a sentence together.

> Is the right conjunction used?

9. The sentence should read:
The kids at our school are much smarter than *the kids* at the other school.

Explanation:

You've got to compare similar things. We call this a problem of **apples and oranges.** Always compare apples to apples and oranges to oranges. (Here, you've got to compare kids to kids, not kids to schools.)

10. The sentence should read:
After seeing the new movie, *the group* decided that Daniel Day-Lewis was its favorite new star.

Explanation:

This is a **misplaced modifier.** The opening phrase "after seeing the new movie" describes what "the group" did, not Daniel Day-Lewis. To avoid ambiguity, modifiers should be as close to what they modify as possible.

11. The sentence should read:
The news stories were *incredible*.

Explanation:

Word choice is the problem here. We'll cover some common **word choice** mistakes later on.

12. The sentence should read:
The meeting is scheduled for 4:00 P.M.

Explanation:

This is an error from the school of **redundancy:** 4:00 P.M. means "four o'clock in the afternoon." It's not necessary to say both.

13. The sentence should read:
That is to say, *it is* the way you asked for it.

Explanation:

As written, this is a **sentence fragment**. Standing on its own, it makes no sense because it has neither a subject nor a verb.

14. The sentence should read:
I have scarcely any money to spend.

Explanation:

"Don't have scarcely any" is a **double negative.** Don't never use none, okay?

15. The sentence should read:
Of the fifteen people at the party, Marielle is the *most* beautiful.

Explanation:

Different words must be used when **comparing** two things, and when **comparing** three or more things. Marielle is the *more* beautiful of the two; she is the *most* beautiful of the fifteen.

16. The sentence should read:
She was running so *quickly* that I couldn't catch her.

Explanation:

Here, an adjective (quick) was used to describe a verb (running). You need an *adverb*. It is an **adjective/adverb** error.

Is an adjective or an adverb required?

17. The sentence should read:
    Dominick told Henry that *Dominick* couldn't finish the job.

Explanation:

We know. That sounds awful. But as the sentence was written, the pronoun *he* was **ambiguous**. Strictly speaking, it could have referred to Dominick or Henry.

Does the pronoun *clearly* refer to the noun?

Phew! That seems like a lot of stuff to absorb. But don't worry. We'll go through each type of mistake one by one and cover the most common way it shows up on the test. By the time you've finished the chapter, you'll be a grammar whiz.

TENSE

It is not necessary to write sentences solely in one tense. Action can shift from the past, to the present, to the future.

> *"He was a great man; he is remembered for what he would have become."*

See, lots of tenses in one coherent sentence.

What does need to happen is that tenses must *make sense* in the context of the sentence. If I tell you I did something last year, then my actions took place in the past tense.

For our purposes, you need to recognize three types of past:
1. The plain old past.

> *"She took the test."*

2. The past that took place recently and over a period of time.

> *"Over the past year, she has been taking tests."*

3. The past that took place before something else in the past. It uses "had" to describe the past of the past, and is always used with the simple past.

There are three tenses to describe the past.

> *"Before she took the SAT last year, she had never taken any tests."*

HOW TO SPOT A TENSE ERROR

No problem. There are a couple of things to watch out for. First, keep an eye out for the unusual verb forms, like *to lie* and *to swim*. Next, watch out for the odd verb tenses. Remember some basic rules:

> *To lie means to lie down.*

> *To lay means to put or to place.*

BUT, the past tense of "to lie" is "lay." So . . .

> *"I am going to lie down, and yesterday I lay down for a nap."*

For strange verbs, which you may not be certain of, see if you can find a familiar verb that is similar.

You may not be sure if Mary *had swum* or *had swam*, but you may know that she *had run* last week. (You wouldn't say that she *had ran*, would you?)

The last thing to remember is the conditional form. That's the verb form you'd use to express a wish or something that is conditional on something else. It usually takes the form "*If* something *were* true, it *would* be wonderful.":

> "If *I* were *class president, I would give free lunches to all.*"

Why does ETS test these forms? Because they are the most common mistakes made in spoken English. Before reading this book, you might have missed this type of error; now you'll know what to look for.

TENSE DRILL

Try the following drill. Correct the verbs that are in the wrong tense, in the context of the sentence. Some are correct as written. Take special note of some of the odd verbs like *to swim*, and *to lie*, which have strange-sounding past tenses. Then check the answer key on page 93.

1. Today, I will *lay*/*lie* in the sun.

2. Yesterday, I *lay*/*lie* in the sun.

3. Last week, Mary *swam*/*swum* in the school swim meet.

4. Before she swam in the race last week, Mary *had swam*/*had swum* in only one other race.

5. The wasp *stang*/*stung* her when she hit the nest.

6. If I *was*/*were* going with you, I'd be happy.

7. If you had come home, you *had*/*would have* found the message.

8. Last year, he *would have spoken*/*would speak* if you had asked.

9. The night the story broke, the phone *rung*/*rang* constantly.

10. If I *was*/*were* a rich man, I would learn to speak better English.

SUBJECT-VERB AGREEMENT

The subject of the sentence must agree with the verb. Namely, if there is a singular subject the verb must be singular. If there is a plural subject, the verb must be plural.

That's the easy part.

The hard part is twofold.

Sidebar notes

Watch out for verbs such as *to lie* and *to swim* as well as the conditional verb form.

A singular subject must have a singular verb; a plural subject must have a plural verb.

Part One: You must decide what the subject is

This may sound easy, but your pals at ETS like to keep the subject as far from the verb as possible. How can they do that? Simple. They can throw in lots of distracting modifying phrases to throw you off. Cross them out and you'll be amazed at how clear the answer becomes. Hence:

> *"The number ~~of dollars necessary to buy~~ groceries for ~~the average group of ten people~~ are in excess of two hundred."*

This may seem confusing, but hunt around. Cross off prepositional phrases before the verb and the sentence becomes:

> *"The* number are *in excess of two hundred."*

Now it's much simpler to decipher that the subject "the number" and verb "are" do not agree.

Part Two: You must figure out if the subject is singular or plural

This may sound easy, but it's not. ETS loves to test you with nouns that sound plural but are really singular.

The following is a list of singular pronouns:

Anybody, anyone

Nobody, no one, neither, none

One

Somebody, someone

Everybody, everyone, either, each

You can remember them by the acronym **A NOSE**.

Even though, technically, some of these can function as either plural or singular, depending on the context in which they are used, ETS almost always tests them as singular, because that's how they're almost always misused.

Collective nouns are also singular.

A partial list of tricky singular nouns is as follows:

> The number
> The amount
> The audience
> The group
> The XYZ Corporation
> America (or any city, state, or country)

Linking two subjects with "and" makes the subject plural; linking with "or" makes it singular.

> *"Mary **and** I* are *going to the show."*

Sidebar notes:

ETS likes to separate the subject from the verb by using lots of modifying phrases.

Pronouns such as *anyone*, *none*, *everybody*, and *either* are singular.

Collective nouns such as *the number*, *the group*, and *the United States* are singular.

*"Paul **or** Jim is going to the show."*

Watch out for subjects that have "and" but are really expressing *one thing*.

"Gin and tonic is what my aunt drinks."

"Rock and roll is here to stay."

"Peanut butter and jelly is my favorite lunch."

How Do I Recognize Subject-Verb Errors?

Another easy assignment. First, bracket all prepositional phrases that lie between the subject and the verb. They are distractors, and reading the sentence without them will help you focus.

Second, watch out for any sentence in which you see the ambiguous pronouns or collective nouns that are listed above. Chances are, you're going to be tested on subject-verb agreement.

Keep clear and focused: find the subject, and decide if it's singular or plural.

Subject-Verb Drill

1. None of us *is/are* going to the concert.

2. Either Nirvana or Pearl Jam *are/is* a great choice for the dance.

3. One of the kids from the new school *are/is* going to win the championship.

4. This group of people *is/are* friendly once you get to know them.

5. Mary Jo and Beth, two of the members of the team, *is/are* the best ones to ask.

6. Neither my mother nor my father *know/knows* anything about that.

7. Either Mark or Pete, two of the nicest guys I know, *was/were* winning the debate.

8. Everyone in the senior class *want/wants* to have that song for the prom theme.

9. Either Madonna or Michael Jackson *are/is* the highest-paid performer around.

10. Supply and demand *are/is* taught in economics classes around the world.

Answers are on page 93.

PRONOUN AGREEMENT

What's wrong with this sentence?

> *"Anyone who goes to college knows they are in for the best four years of their life."*

A pronoun must agree in terms of number and gender with the noun it replaces.

Sounds good, doesn't it?

There's only one problem—it's not. "Anyone" is singular (remember?), so when you replace it in a sentence, you must replace it with a singular pronoun. This is one of the most common mistakes in spoken English because the choices are so stilted-sounding—"he or she," or, "he" or "she." None really sounds quite right. So "they" and "their" become great cop-outs for correct form. "They are" is fine when you talk to your friends, but with ETS, watch out for those singular subjects.

HOW DO I SPOT A PRONOUN AGREEMENT ERROR?

Keep an eye on those pronouns that come up later in the sentence. Ask yourself what noun or pronoun they might be referring to. Be especially cautious when one of those ambiguous singular pronouns is floating around (more about them next).

PRONOUN AGREEMENT DRILL

For each of the following, decide which pronoun is appropriate. You can check your answers on page 93.

Watch out for pronouns.

1. Each of the women fought for *their/her* rights.

2. When one has to go to school, *one/you* should be prepared.

3. If the guidance department tells you to do that, *they/it* must be crazy.

4. When the school newspaper staff writes an editorial, *it is/they are* always right on the mark.

5. If Jeannie and Kathryn go, *she/they* will certainly win the best-dressed prize.

6. Anyone who goes to Montreal will feel as if *he is/they are* visiting Europe.

7. One thing everyone knows about television news is that *they're/it's* biased.

8. The jury was sequestered until *they/it* reached a verdict.

9. Nobody who goes to that store thinks *they/she* is getting a bargain.

10. The program has assisted the citizens in getting *his/their* needed improvements.

PRONOUN CASE

No, it's not the place where you keep your pronouns.

Pronoun case refers to the form of the pronoun you need in a sentence. When do you use *I* and when do you use *me*?

> *"He brought the book to Martha and I."*

A good way to check this is to cross out "Martha and" and end up with

> *"He brought the book to I."*

Now, that sounds wrong.

The pronouns *I, you, he, she, we,* and *who* are subject pronouns. You use them to perform the action in the sentence. The recipient of the actions, however, is going to be an object pronoun such as *me, him, her, us,* and *whom*.

Another place where you may find pronouns used incorrectly is where you are comparing two things.

Which is correct?

> *"Bruno is nicer than* her."

or

> *"Bruno is nicer than* she."

Believe it or not, it should be the second: "Bruno is nicer than she." Why? When you are making a comparison, you are implying "is": "Bruno is nicer than *she is.*" Strange, but true.

The last thing to watch out for is a possessive pronoun.

Which is correct?

> *"My mother is happy about* me *going to college."*

or

> *"My mother is happy about* my *going to college."*

Again, the second one is correct. My mother is not really happy about *me*. What she's happy about is the fact that I'm going to college or *"my going to college."*

HOW DO I SPOT A PRONOUN CASE ERROR?

By now you should be catching on to the idea that it would probably behoove you to check pronouns in all sentences. There's a lot that could be wrong with them. Remember some of the most common traps, and you'll be ten steps ahead of the game.

The form of a pronoun depends on how it is used: for example, a subject (*he*), an object (*him*), and a possessive (*his*).

PRONOUN CASE DRILL

Watch out for pronouns.

1. I want to give the present to Paul and *he/him*.

2. The speaker, about *who/whom* we were so excited, never showed up.

3. After going to the city, Mary and *she/her* wanted to live there.

4. Paulette says she is worried about *me/my* gaining weight.

5. This dedication is for *whom/who*?

6. Charlotte is better than *her/she* at painting.

7. As we went to the concert, we wondered what had happened to *she/her*.

8. Martin is better than *I/me* at this particular game.

9. If you and *I/me* take this test, we'll both do well.

10. Just between you and *I/me*, I want to go to the dance.

Check your answers on page 93.

IDIOMS

What are idioms? They are the way we put words together by convention—rather than any real rule.

For example, you would say:

There are no "rules" for idioms.

> *"I am different* from *you"*

rather than

> *"I am different* about *you."*

Here, you must rely on your ear to pick up an expression that doesn't sound right. If a preposition or prepositional phrase is underlined, that's a good place to start looking.

HOW DO I SPOT AN IDIOM ERROR?

Usually, it's the last resort when a sentence *sounds* wrong, but you can't put your finger on it. Check the prepositional phrases. If you're still not sure, then pull the phrase out of the sentence and try it on its own. Often, without that confused rambling sentence around it, it becomes clear what the problem is.

IDIOM DRILL

Fill in the correct preposition.

1. We agreed __on__ the theme for the school dance.

2. We argued __about__ the subject for hours in class.

3. He lives __in__ New York.

4. He lives __at__ the Park Plaza Hotel.

5. He lives __on__ Fifty-ninth Street.

6. I am concerned __about__ your score on the test.

7. She is delighted __with__ the new dress.

8. My mother is impatient __with__ me.

9. A passport is necessary __for__ travel outside the United States.

10. I am confident __about__ my ability to take the test.

Answers are on page 93.

PARALLELISM

Whenever you're expressing a series of ideas or actions, you should make them parallel in form. That's the rule. Now, what does that mean?

> *"The enclosed resume indicates that I am interested in writing, editing, and I like to read."*

Good luck—this person will not get the job. The correct form should read:

> *"The enclosed resume indicates that I am interested in writing, editing, and reading."*

You're listing three things that you are good at; therefore, they must be in the same format.

Watch out for sentences that are crowded with lots of other information. Dig out the items or actions that are being listed. Again, training your eye and your ear to cross out those extraneous details will really help you zero in on the error in the sentence.

HOW DO I SPOT A PARALLELISM ERROR?

Just keep an eye out anytime there is a list of things in a sentence. Be especially careful when there are two or three things that a person or group is trying to do and there are lots of distracting phrases tossed in between those actions. Make sure they're in the same form, and you'll be all set.

PARALLELISM DRILL

Here, underline the part of the sentence that is not parallel in structure, and correct it if you like.

1. Johanna read the book, summarized its contents, and ~~submit-ting~~ *submitted* it to the teacher.

2. When reading the paper, I enjoy perusing the comics, glancing at Ann Landers, and ~~skip~~ *skipping* the sports.

3. Marcia was ~~thrilled~~ *shopped*—she bought tickets to the Madonna concert, ~~shopping~~ for a new outfit, and read the latest biography of Princess Diana.

4. The administration issued an ultimatum to the student body: no smoking, no drinking, and ~~they couldn't have~~ *no* visitors after 12:00 A.M.

5. The peer counselor listened intently and ~~with compassion~~ *compassionly*.

6. The class will cover the basics of English: ~~good writing~~ *to write well*, to comprehend what is written, and to learn to discriminate between what is correct and incorrect.

7. When Eileen came home from school, she loved to go running, to shower, and ~~doing~~ *to do* her homework before dinner.

8. To call the Screaming Blue Banshees the best new band in town is like ~~calling~~ *to call* my sister the best-looking girl.

9. Whenever I go camping, I really enjoy swimming, ~~to hike~~ *hiking*, and cooking over the campfire.

10. The kids decided that for their Halloween party they would bob for apples, go trick-or-treating, and ~~scaring~~ *scare* the other neighborhood kids.

Answers are on page 93.

Watch out for a list or a series.

NOUN AGREEMENT

What's wrong with this sentence?

"Jessica and Jennifer are looking for a summer job."

Unless Jessica and Jennifer intend to get one job and share it, the sentence should read:

"Jessica and Jennifer are looking for summer jobs."

If you have two people, you must have two jobs. Nouns must agree in number with the nouns they are referring to. If you use a pronoun, it also must agree: "John and Soupy drove *their* (not his or her) cars to the party."

A noun must agree with the noun to which it refers.

How Do I Spot a Noun Agreement Error?

Watch out for a noun that refers to another noun.

If you've got nouns referring to each other—just like pronouns—check to make sure that they agree in number. If there is more than one person, there needs to be more than one *thing* for those people.

Noun Agreement Drill

Circle the noun or nouns that do not agree.

1. Of the ten who applied for membership, only three were inducted as a member of the Hall of Fame.

2. When visiting Japan, tourists should be sure to eat at his or her favorite restaurant.

3. The people in that group always look for a deal when shopping.

4. These different vitamins all come in a different jar.

5. James and David will be my best friend.

Compare your answers with those on page 93.

Conjunctions

Conjunctions such as and *and* or *link parts of a sentence together.*

Conjunctions are words that link parts of a sentence together. Some common conjunctions are *and, but, or, because, since, if, that, which, who, either, neither, yet,* and *so.*

Problems arise when the wrong conjunction renders the sentence senseless.

How Do I Spot a Conjunction Error?

Conjunction errors are kind of like idiom errors. The sentence *sounds* kind of funny, but you can't put your finger on it. If there are any of the above-mentioned conjunctions in the sentence, just ask yourself if it couldn't be that it's linking the sentence together in an odd way that doesn't make sense.

Another tricky point ETS will try to catch you on is the use of *that* versus *which.* The rule of thumb is, if a comma can be inserted, you should use *which.* If you're shaky on the use of commas, just remember: a phrase using "which" could be deleted from a sentence without changing its basic meaning; a phrase using "that" gives such important information, its removal would alter the sentence.

Use that *to describe a specific item. Use* which *to describe an item in general.*

> *"Bill needs the book* that *he left on the table."*

Here, Bill is asking for a particular book.

> *"Bill asked for his book,* which *he had left on the table."*

The book in this sentence could be one of many books.

CONJUNCTION DRILL

Circle what you think the proper conjunction should be.

Watch out for something that *sounds* wrong.

1. The reason for his lateness was *because/that* he had a doctor's appointment.

2. I am going to the play with my cousin *and he is/who is* coming from the suburbs.

3. I like bananas, *that/which* are high in potassium.

4. I followed the instructions to the letter, *and/but* I still got most of the questions wrong.

Answers are on page 94.

APPLES AND ORANGES

You know the saying—you can't compare apples and oranges. The same is true in a sentence. Try this for an example.

> *"I always like reading the stories of Edgar Allan Poe more than Stephen King when I want a good scare."*

The problem? We're comparing the stories of Edgar Allan Poe to Stephen King himself. What we mean to do is compare stories to stories.

Two things being compared must, in fact, be comparable.

> *"I always like reading the stories of Edgar Allan Poe more than* the stories of *Stephen King when I want a good scare."*

or, we could also say:

> *"I always like reading the stories of Edgar Allan Poe more than* those of *Stephen King when I want a good scare."*

HOW DO I SPOT AN APPLES AND ORANGES ERROR?

Easy! Always be wary of comparisons. These are easy to miss if you don't know what you're looking for. If you're comparing things, make sure you're comparing apples with apples—or nouns with nouns, actions with actions.

APPLES AND ORANGES DRILL

Watch out for a comparison.

Try your hand at spotting the illogical comparisons in the following examples. Rewrite the sentence to make sense.

1. The rules of Scrabble are less complicated than *the rules of* Monopoly, but Scrabble is still a harder game.

2. The people in our office put out much more work than the *people in the* office next door.

3. My dentist's technique is so much more painless than your dentist.*'s technique*

4. The new chemistry teacher says that this textbook is much more up-to-date than last year.*'s textbook*

5. Marissa learned how to cook in China—her cooking is so much better than my mother.*'s cooking*

6. Our school's track team is the league champion; they're completely superior to your school.*'s track team*

7. Cooking with lots of vegetables is healthier than *cooking w/* meat.

8. John's grade on the last test was much lower than the previous test.*grade*

9. Although her dorm room was nice, it wasn't nearly as nice as her friend.*'s room*

10. Carol wanted to be a teacher, just like her mother *was/wanted to be a*

Answers are on page 94.

MISPLACED MODIFIERS

Look at this sentence:

> *"Driving down Highway 101, the rain pelted my car."*

Who was driving? Me or the rain?

A modifier is a describing word or phrase. In this sentence, the phrase "Driving down Highway 101" is meant to describe me, not the rain. To avoid any ambiguity in written English, the modifier must always be placed as close as possible to the word or words it modifies. Here, for example, either

A modifier must be as close as possible to the word(s) it describes.

> *"As I drove down Highway 101, my car was pelted by the rain."*

or

> *"The rain pelted my car as I drove down Highway 101."*

It may seem like a nitpicky difference to you, and it probably is, in *spoken* English. But in written English, the rules call for precision. And for the purposes of this test, close doesn't count. So, when you're looking for an error, always check modifiers to be sure they're next to what they're modifying.

How Do I Spot a Misplaced Modifier Error?

Watch out, first of all, for sentences that begin with modifying phrases. Anything that starts out with a phrase followed by a comma should be checked to be sure that the word it describes immediately follows that comma.

Keep in mind the general rule: Modifiers should be as close as possible to the word or words they modify.

> Watch out for sentences that start with a long, descriptive phrase followed by a comma.

Misplaced Modifier Drill

Correct each sentence below.

1. To pass English this year, a strict adherence to the rules of grammar must be followed.

   For me to pass English ... I must
   follow a

2. Applying sunscreen with an SPF of 15, sunburn was still inevitable for Sinead.

3. When she was six, Carla's mother totaled the family car.

4. After returning to Kansas from that wild trip to Oz, the farm was boring for poor old Dorothy.

5. Even though he was the best man for the job, my boss overlooked Evan.

    _____

    _____

    _____

6. To ensure the best possible protection, life insurance policies are recommended for homeowners.

    _____

    _____

    _____

7. Upon close inspection, the diamond ring was discovered to be a well-made fake.

    _____

    _____

    _____

8. After taking her SAT II: Writing Subject Test, college was definitely in the picture for Gwen.

    _____

    _____

    _____

9. Although he never had much success at basketball, the final point was scored by Paul.

    _____

    _____

    _____

Check your answers on page 94.

WORD CHOICE

Some of these errors will be simple and almost look like spelling errors. Keep an eye out for them. Others have to do with words that are frequently misused.
    For example, what's wrong with this sentence?

> *"Whenever I go shopping at the Gap, I get loads of complements on my outfit."*

It looks perfect, doesn't it? Or did you notice that the word *complement* was wrong? Complement with an *e* means to complete, like complementary colors. Compl*i*ment with an *i* means to praise, which is clearly what was intended here.

Some common word choice errors are as follows:

Word choice errors concern the proper use of a word.

Your/You're

Your is the possessive form of you—"*Your* house is nice." *You're* is a contraction of the two words *you* and *are*. Use it to mean "you are." "*You're* invited to the party."

Their/They're

Same as above. *Their* is possessive—"*Their* car is nicer than your car." *They're* is a contraction of *they* and *are*. "*They're* the nicest people."

Affect/Effect

Affect means to influence. I *affect* the situation I'm in. *Effect* is usually a noun meaning "the result." It could also be a verb meaning "to accomplish."

> "*The* effect *was stunning in the movie.*"

or

> "*The new principal hopes to* effect *changes in the school schedules.*"

Bring/Take

You *bring* something to the person who is speaking; you *take* away from the person who is speaking.

> "Bring *me the book.*"

> "Take *this home.*"

Borrow/Lend

You *borrow* from; you *lend* to.

> "*I'm* borrowing *this from the library.*"

> "*I'll* lend *you my skirt.*"

Fewer/Less

Fewer refers to things that can be counted.

> "*I have* fewer *french fries.*"

Less refers to things that cannot be counted.

> "*I have* less *mashed potatoes.*"

Make sure you use the right quantity words for countable nouns and noncountable nouns (e.g., *fewer* vs. *less*, *number* vs. *amount*).

(Remember this when your teacher asks for "five pages or less." That's wrong. It should be "five pages or fewer.")

Number/Amount
Same thing. *Number* for stuff that can be counted. *Amount* for stuff that can't.

> *"I have a* number *of dollars, but an* amount *of money."*

Principal/Principle
The *principal* as a noun is the head of the school, or money that earns interest. If it's used as an adjective, it means "the main or most important." The *principle* is "the rule" or "fundamental truth." (Remember that your princi*pal* is your *pal*.)

> *"My* principal *urged me to adhere to higher* principles
> *and to stop cheating."*

Stationery/Stationary
Stationery with an *e* goes in an envelope (with an *e*—get it?). *Stationary* with an *a* means to stay in one place.

Aggravate/Irritate
Aggravate means to make worse. It is often used incorrectly when *irritate* is meant. You do not *aggravate* your mother, you *irritate* her. (Point that out next time she's yelling—it's really irritating.) You can only *aggravate* a situation (i.e., make it worse). Isn't this irritating?

HOW DO I SPOT A WORD CHOICE ERROR?

Watch out for a word that looks misspelled.

If a word looks misspelled, it may be a word choice problem. If you're not good at these, you may want to start a list of commonly misused and confused words to memorize. There really aren't that many on the test, so don't worry too much about them. The fun thing is that when you do spot one, it's easily corrected.

WORD CHOICE DRILL
Choose the correct word.

1. Our legal system believes that criminals should be *persecuted/prosecuted*.
2. The special effects were *incredible/incredulous*.
3. He is an *eminent/imminent* person in the field.
4. He made *allusions/illusions* to patriotism in his speech.
5. We would have *less/fewer* people than we expected.
6. I could *accept/except* the fact that we were not going.

Answers are on page 94.

REDUNDANCY

Redundancy is when you say things again and repeat them. What's the problem with that sentence? To say things again means to repeat them. If words are unnecessary because they were already stated in a sentence, they are wrong. Watch out for redundancies. The sentences in the drill will probably sound familiar. These are phrases that people use all the time.

Redundancy means stating something already stated.

How Do I Spot a Redundancy Error?

If a sentence sounds very wordy, it may be that some of those words are redundant. If you can remove words without altering the meaning one bit, then those words are *redundant*.

Redundancy Drill

Cross out the words that are redundant.

1. The reason I want to go to the dance is because John is there.
2. Let's go at 2:00 A.M. this morning.
3. There's a good chance you will probably want to talk to her.
4. In the year of 1977, Gabrielle danced to the disco beat.
5. The consensus of opinions on this subject is that this test is lame.
6. The polls are way too premature to predict anything.
7. The period of time between Thanksgiving and Christmas is important to retailers.
8. My estimation represented the best approximate guess.
9. I think English, in my opinion, is my best subject.

Watch out for wordy sentences.

Answers are on page 94.

Sentence Fragments

Sentences need a subject and a verb. They must also sound logically complete.

> *"Since I want to become a doctor."*

Since you want to become a doctor, *what*? This is a fragment. Sometimes you simply need to add a word. Sometimes, as here, removing a word makes it complete.

> *"I want to become a doctor."*

Other times the punctuation can be shifted or altered. Of course, many writers use fragments deliberately to create a desired effect. You may even do so in your own writing. ETS writers, however, do not use fragments.

A sentence must have both a main subject and a main verb.

How Do I Spot Fragment Errors?

Careful reading almost always gives these away. You can rely on your ear. If you're not sure, ask yourself what the subject is and what the verb is. If one's missing (more frequently it is the subject) then your work is done.

Watch out for something that *sounds* wrong.

Fragment Drill

Change the following fragments into complete sentences.

1. Although he wants to come along.

   _____
   _____
   _____

2. Going to the store to buy fruit.

   _____
   _____
   _____

3. Buying CDs for the party.

   _____
   _____
   _____

4. To go to college for four years.

   _____
   _____
   _____

Answers are on page 95.

A double negative is redundant: The two negatives cancel each other out.

Double Negatives

"I can't hardly wait for summer."

What's wrong here? This is kind of like redundancy. Two negatives would technically cancel each other out. Only one is necessary. It would be better to say:

"I can't wait" or *"I can hardly wait."*

Watch out for words such as *hardly* or *scarcely*.

How Do I Spot a Double Negative Problem?

Always be careful if a sentence uses the words "hardly" or "scarcely"; they're the most common double negative traps.

DOUBLE NEGATIVE DRILL

Correct the following sentences.

1. We couldn't scarcely see the movie from our seats.

   _____

   _____

   _____

2. I don't want none of that candy; I'm on a diet.

   _____

   _____

   _____

3. I hadn't been there but two minutes before my mother called.

   _____

   _____

   _____

4. We hadn't hardly any money left after buying the new U2 CD.

   _____

   _____

   _____

Answers are on page 95.

MORE/MOST

"My sister is the best looking of the two of us."

Does that look wrong? Actually, when comparing two things, you have to say *better*. Those "-est" words always refer to comparisons among three or more things.

Some examples are as follows:

Best for three or more—better for two.

Least for three or more—less for two.

Most for three or more—more for two.

Oldest for three or more—older for two.

Among for more than two—between for two.

To compare two things use -*er* words. To compare three things or more use -*est* words.

It's also interesting to note that you can't say something is more unique, more straight, or more perfect. Perfect is perfect; unique is unique. You'd have to say that something is more nearly perfect, or more nearly unique.

HOW DO I SPOT A MORE/MOST PROBLEM?

Again, watch those comparisons. Note if you've got two things or more than two things. Then check the word you've used to describe the comparison.

Watch out for a comparison.

MORE/MOST DRILL

1. Whenever the ten of us go out, Joan is the *loudest/louder*.
2. Marta is the *prettiest/prettier* twin.
3. Of my twenty sisters, Jane is the *eldest/elder*.
4. Choose *between/among* these four colors.
5. After seeing all of Woody Allen's movies, I found *Husbands and Wives* to be the *most/more* revealing.

Answers are on page 95.

ADJECTIVE/ADVERB

Adjectives describe nouns. Adverbs describe verbs, adjectives, or other adverbs.

When you're describing an action, an adverb, or an adjective, you need an adverb.

> *"You should do* good *on the test."*

Not if it's an English test. Since we're describing how you will do, an adverb is needed. The sentence should read:

> *"You should do* well *on the test."*

HOW DO I SPOT AN ADJECTIVE/ADVERB ERROR?

Check your describing words and ask what other word or words they may be describing. It's more common to use an adjective when you need an adverb than the other way around.

ADJECTIVE/ADVERB DRILL

1. John went to the store *quick/quickly*.
2. The job is *good/well* for her.
3. The questions on the test are *easy/easily*.
4. The questions on the test are *easy/easily* answered.

Answers are on page 95.

Watch out for modifiers.

AMBIGUITY

> *"Mary told Alicia that* she *would certainly do well on the SAT."*

Is Mary bragging or being nice? The pronoun *she* is ambiguous here. This is a sticky one. In spoken English, this kind of ambiguity is okay. The way you tilt your head or gesture or use your voice is often enough to clear up any misunderstanding. If that fails, your friends can say "Huh?" In written English, the rules are more strict. Technically, you would have to say:

> *"Mary told Alicia that* Mary *would certainly do well on the SAT."*

or

> *"Mary told Alicia that* Alicia *would certainly do well on the SAT."*

Sounds bad, doesn't it? That's what makes it such a good right answer. Anyone who doesn't really know the rules would never pick it.

A pronoun must *clearly* refer to the noun it replaces.

HOW DO I SPOT AN AMBIGUITY ERROR?

As always—*watch those pronouns*. If it is even conceivable that a pronoun could refer to more than one thing in a sentence, you've found the mistake.

AMBIGUITY DRILL

Circle the ambiguous word or words in each sentence.

1. Paul told David to help him with the dishes and he had a fit.

2. David asked Paul when the last time was that he helped with any chores.

3. Paul told David that he swept the floor, cleaned the car, and raked the leaves, which was not his job.

4. David yelled at Paul until his father came into the room and punished him.

5. David made up with Paul, and he apologized for the unpleasantness.

Watch out for pronouns.

Answers are on page 95.

THE FINAL WORD ON GRAMMAR

This seems like a lot of information to process, but keep in mind that you probably recognized some of these errors from the very beginning. Concentrate on your weak spots. There will be plenty of drills in the next section to help you fine-tune trouble areas.

THE GOOD NEWS

Remember, ETS does *not* test either spelling or punctuation.

Spelling is not tested on the SAT II: Writing Test! We know that some of the word choice errors look like misspellings, but they really aren't. If you see a hard word, don't worry about the spelling. It won't be wrong.

Punctuation is not tested. The only time to worry about punctuation is when you are asked to identify or correct a sentence fragment or a run-on sentence. Semicolons and colons are just fine, even though they look funny.

5

Identifying Sentence Errors

First of all, since we did this way back when, let's review how the test is structured.

Writing Test	
Essay	20 Min. Total
Identifying Sentence Errors—30 questions Improving Sentences—18 questions Improving Paragraphs—12 questions	40 Min. Total

Make sure you remember the structure of the Writing Test.

You'll notice that Identifying Sentence Errors accounts for a total of thirty questions. This makes it the winner in the "Most-Tested Question Format on the Writing Test" contest.

Let's look at what the instructions for the Identifying Sentence Errors section of the test look like:

Directions: The following sentences contain problems in grammar, usage, word choice, and idiom.

Some sentences are correct.
No sentence contains more than one error.

You will find that the error, if there is one, is underlined and lettered. Elements of the sentence that are not underlined will not be changed. In choosing answers, follow the requirements of standard written English.

If there is an error, select the <u>one underlined part</u> that must be changed in order to make the sentence correct and fill in the corresponding oval on the answer sheet.

If there is no error, fill in answer oval E.

Now check out what an Identifying Sentence Errors question looks like.

22. In 1991, <u>after</u> the success of her "Blond Ambition"
         A
tour, Madonna, <u>by signing</u> a new contract <u>with</u>
           B   C
Sony Corporation, <u>has become</u> the most highly
                D
paid female entertainer of the year. <u>No error</u>
                                  E

Not all Identifying Sentence Errors questions have an error.

By the way, the answer to the above question is (D). It was an error in the tense of the verb. If I'm talking about something that happened to Madonna in the past (1991), then I have to say she "became." Of course, the really great thing about this type of question is that you do not have to correct any errors—your job is to locate an error, if one exists. I suppose now is a good time to cover a crucial rule:

In approximately one-fifth of the Identifying Sentence Error questions, the answer will be (E): No error.

This is an important point, because the first instinct you will have is to find an error. Sometimes there just isn't one. We don't mean to imply that out of thirty Identifying Sentence Error questions, you will have exactly six (E)s, but it probably should lie somewhere in the vicinity of five to seven. If there are fewer than that, you're probably finding fault where none exists (and you thought only your teachers could do that). If there are more than eight (E)s, then you probably aren't looking hard enough.

SOME BASIC IDEAS

Before we get started, let's review pacing. As mentioned in the "Cracking the Writing Test" section, sixty questions in forty minutes will probably translate into a lot of careless errors. Slow down, and don't be concerned about answering every single question. Check the pacing chart and decide exactly how many you can comfortably skip. Don't forget, though, that not knowing the right answer does not necessarily mean skipping.

Remember, accuracy is more important than speed. You don't have to answer every question.

PROCESS OF ELIMINATION

Even though it may be hard to find the error, it may be simpler to find choices where there is *no* error.

If I asked you what was wrong with the sentence,

> *"After a hard day at school, Snacksters always hit the spot."*

you might have a problem. But if I underlined four parts of the sentence like this,

> *"After a hard day at school, Snacksters always hit the spot."*

you could probably tell me at least one of the underlined parts that *isn't* wrong. And that leads us back to our BIG IMPORTANT RULE mentioned in chapter 3:

> ANYTIME YOU CAN ELIMINATE EVEN
> ONE WRONG ANSWER, YOU MUST GUESS.

Here, you could eliminate "after," "at," and "the spot." "Snacksters" is incorrect—as written it is modified by "After a hard day at school."

Since it is almost always possible to eliminate one wrong answer, you can almost always guess. The only time you should leave something blank is when it simply isn't possible, due to time constraints, to even read the question.

THE ORDER IN WHICH YOU SHOULD DO THE SECTIONS

Identifying Sentence Errors is the quickest section to do. Number one, it's usually simple to quickly eliminate at least one or two obvious parts of the sentence that are right (and, therefore, wrong answer choices). Number two, it moves more quickly than the other two sections. There's a lot less reading and thinking involved, and the less of that you have to do on any test, the better.

Do Identifying Sentence Errors questions first. All you have to do is spot the error; you don't have to correct it.

> Do all the Identifying Sentence Errors questions **first**.

Remember, however, that the questions within the sections do not go in order of difficulty, so always be on your toes. The last questions may have easy answers, and the first ones may be the ones you need to guess on.

SOME GENERAL TEST-TAKING TIPS FOR IDENTIFYING SENTENCE ERRORS QUESTIONS

Tip number one may seem ridiculously obvious, but as is often the case with ridiculous statements, it's important.

> **TIP NUMBER ONE:**
> Parts of the sentence that are not underlined are always correct.

Don't forget about the five most common error types.

Don't waste precious time reading those parts too closely unless they shed some light on the rest of the sentence. Often they are distractors. This leads us to:

> **TIP NUMBER TWO:**
> Bracket prepositional phrases and filler. Get down to the nitty-gritty of the sentence.

Go through some of the basic questions that will help you zero in on errors:

- What's the subject?
- What's the verb?
- Do subject and verb match?
- Are any pronouns underlined?
    —Are they in the proper case?
    —Do they agree with the nouns they replace?
    —Are they ambiguous?
- Is there a comparison taking place?
    —Is ETS comparing apples and oranges?
    —Is one of the more/most words underlined?
- Is there an adverb/adjective underlined?

- Are any of those weird word choice words underlined?

- Any words that could be idiomatically incorrect?

- Double negatives?

- Words that are redundant?

- Is it a fragment?

AGGRESSIVENESS DRILL

Go through these sentences and bracket any phrases that are there to distract you. See if you can eliminate even one wrong answer.

1. The sooner the <u>audience</u>, which was <u>composed</u> of
             A   B

   myriad different types of people, <u>were able</u> to
                                   C

   appreciate the music, the sooner the orchestra,

   which <u>came from Serbia</u>, was able to enjoy
                  D

   itself. <u>No error</u>
        E

   C

2. Martina <u>was able</u> to play a good game, <u>despite the crowd</u>,
          A   B

   which yelled and <u>screamed</u> throughout the
                    C

   match <u>for a better</u> line referee. <u>No error</u>
         D   E

   E

3. Something <u>must be done</u> about the <u>rapid spreading</u>
             A   B

   notion that politicians are nothing <u>but a bunch of</u>
                                  C

   crooked cheats who run the country for <u>their</u>
                             D

   own personal gain. <u>No error</u>
           E

   B

4. <u>Using periodicals</u> for research is recommended to
      A

   the student, whether <u>working</u> in a group with others
                    B

   or alone, <u>who expect</u> good grades and wants to go far
           C

   in <u>his education.</u> <u>No error</u>
     D   E

   C

Answers are on page 95.

How did you do? On the first example, were you able to ignore the phrase "which was composed of myriad different types of people" to zero in on the error (C)? The subject is "audience," which makes the verb "were" incorrect. The sentence should read "the audience . . . was able. . . ." Did you eliminate (A) as a possible choice? What could be wrong with the word *audience*? Let's look at the next example.

Example two can be taken apart and checked piece by piece. The first half states "Martina was able to play . . ." Ignore the "a good game" part, and you'll see that there's nothing that could be wrong with these words. Eliminate choice (A). The next phrase "despite the crowd" simply describes how she was able to play. Looks harmless enough. Eliminate choice (B). Chances are if "yelled," a non-underlined part of the question is good, then "screamed" must be fine as well. Eliminate (C). At this point you have a fifty-fifty chance of a correct answer. Nothing really looks wrong with "for a better." Run through your checklist, and TRUST YOURSELF. The answer is (E)!

The next example has lots of distractions. Let's get rid of some answer choices quickly. Both "must be done" and "but a bunch of" look harmless enough. This sentence has both an adverb/adjective combination and a juicy pronoun. Concentrate on them. The pronoun is the faster of the two to check. To what does it refer? "Their" refers to "politicians," so the reference is correct. It replaces a plural noun—"politicians"—with a plural pronoun—"their." Let's look at "rapid" and "increasing." "Increasing" describes the notion. That looks fine. "Rapid" describes "increasing." A word that describes an adjective must be an adverb. It should be "the rapidly increasing notion." If you chose (B), then you were right.

Use a two-pass system on the Identifying Sentence Errors questions. Do the easy ones first and then go back to the hard ones.

Last but not least, let's examine example number four. First eliminate the distracting phrase "whether working in a group with others or alone." Doing this shows you immediately that "who expect" goes with "student." Would you say "the student expect"? That sounds funny. The problem is that the subject—"student"—and the verb—"expect"—do not agree. It should read "the student expects." Making a quick check of the pronoun "his" shows that it refers to "student," which is correct. The answer is (C).

This may seem like a lot of work at first, but as you practice, you will become proficient at moving quickly through Identifying Sentence Errors.

QUICK IDENTIFYING SENTENCE ERRORS WRAP-UP

- ◆ Do the Identifying Sentence Errors questions first.

- ◆ On a first pass, skip the ones that look very hard.

- ◆ Run through your checklist of possible errors. Concentrate on verbs, pronouns, and modifying phrases. Check for comparisons, conjunctions, and idioms.

- ◆ TRUST YOURSELF! Don't hesitate to pick (E) sometimes.

IDENTIFYING SENTENCE ERRORS DRILL

Try your hand at the following questions. Remember, some will be correct as written. The best part about Identifying Sentence Errors is that you don't need to correct the error, just spot it. But for the sake of practice, see if you can correct the errors you find.

1. One of the two people who applied for the
   A   B

   job are going to get hired because we need
          C

   a new worker. No error
        D   E

   C

2. The Halloween party was a great success: the
                     A

   children enjoyed bobbing for apples, playing party
            B   C

   games, and to put costumes on. No error
                D   E

   D

3. The author about whom I wrote my report
                    A

   was recently added to the ten best writers list in
       B   C

   the Sunday magazine. No error
       D   E

   E

4. Just between you and I, *Independence Day* was the
           A   B

   coolest movie I have ever seen. No error
   C   D   E

   A

5. We found out later that it was he who had set off
      A   B   C

   the firecrackers in the principal's office. No error
                    D   E

   E

6. While taking the English SAT II, the pencil that
   A   B

   Ali had borrowed from her sister broke. No error
       C   D   E

   B

7. For days and days, rocking back and forth,
   A   B

   leaving the crew sick and exhausted from
                    C

   their voyage. No error
        D   E

   E

8. Despite the poor weather, I was planning, with my
   A   B   C

   sister, on attending the festival. No error
           D   E

   D

9. Although Audrey thought that <u>she had</u> studied

                                    A

    diligently, she still <u>hadn't</u> scarcely <u>any time</u> left

                             B   C

    <u>to finish</u> the exam. <u>No error</u>

       D   E

10. After Karen used all of <u>her stationary</u> to complete

                              A

    the thank-you <u>notes that</u> she <u>had needed to write</u>,

                    B   C

    she mailed <u>them</u> immediately. <u>No error</u>

                D   E

11. You <u>may think</u> that you are taller <u>than I</u>, but you

         A   B

    are <u>sadly mistaken</u>. <u>No error</u>

    C   D   E

12. <u>Many young adults</u> find it extremely difficult

            A

    <u>to return</u> home from college and <u>abide with</u> the rules

       B   C

    set down by <u>their parents</u>. <u>No error</u>

              D   E

13. <u>Of all</u> the days we got <u>for vacation</u>, the first <u>was</u>

    A   B   C

    by far the <u>most perfect</u>. <u>No error</u>

              D   E

14. Because <u>their</u> class <u>was going</u> on a field trip that

            A   B

    day, James and Alice <u>each</u> needed <u>a lunch</u> to bring to

                      C   D

    school. <u>No error</u>

          E

15. She <u>would never</u> admit it, but Marie <u>was definitely</u>

          A   B

    upset <u>about me</u> getting the seats for the concert before

         C

    <u>she did</u>. <u>No error</u>

      D   E

16. <u>Everyone</u> on the cheerleading squad <u>debated whether</u>

        A   B

    to attempt <u>to learn</u> the new cheers for <u>their routine</u>.

             C   D

    <u>No error</u>

    E

17. I <u>recently heard</u> an announcement <u>where</u> the Rangers
           A   B
will <u>be playing</u> a game at home <u>this weekend</u>.
        C   D
<u>No error</u>
  E

18. Though the <u>assignment called</u> for ten pages or <u>less,</u>
               A   B
Alice found that <u>she needed</u> fifteen pages to convey
                  C
<u>her</u> ideas properly. <u>No error</u>
 D   E

19. The increase in the <u>number</u> of cigarette
                 A
advertisements aimed <u>at young</u> people <u>is a call</u> to
                   B   C
action for antismoking groups <u>around the country</u>.
                             D
<u>No error</u>
  E

20. <u>Since some</u> proponents of the plan <u>are convinced</u>
       A   B
that it will <u>bring employment</u> to the area, others
             C
remain skeptical <u>of the plan's</u> benefits. <u>No error</u>
             D   E

21. Newspaper publishers <u>have united</u> to fight pollution
                 A
<u>by</u> developing <u>one</u> that uses <u>less paper</u>. <u>No error</u>
 B   C   D   E

22. <u>Although</u> Mr. Jones is not <u>as strict as</u> he once was,
    A   B
<u>his class</u> is still a hurdle to overcome <u>when going</u>
  C   D
through high school. <u>No error</u>
             E

23. <u>There are</u> no rules <u>more</u> complicated <u>than chess</u>; it
    A   B   C
can take years to master <u>all the nuances</u> of the game.
                   D
<u>No error</u>
  E

E 24. Susie's ability <u>for supervising</u> was put <u>to the test</u>
                           A   B
<u>recently</u> when she <u>was asked</u> to watch the baby.
   C   D
<u>No error</u>
   E

D 25. The class took <u>offense</u> at the <u>teacher's comments</u>, but
                        A   B
<u>could dispute</u> neither the claim itself <u>or</u> the historical
      C   D
significance of it. <u>No error</u>
                        E

Answers are on pages 95-96.

6

Improving Sentences

Before we begin discussing Improving Sentences, let's take a moment to read the instructions as they appear on the exam.

Directions: In each of the following sentences, some part or all of the sentence is underlined. Below each sentence you will find five ways of phrasing the underlined part. Select the answer that produces the most effective sentence, one that is clear and exact, without awkwardness or ambiguity, and fill in the corresponding oval on your answer sheet. In choosing answers, follow the requirements of standard written English. Choose the answer that best expresses the meaning of the original sentence.

Answer (A) is always the same as the underlined part. Choose answer (A) if you think the original sentence needs no revision.

Now, let's find out what an Improving Sentences question looks like.

Unlike Identifying Sentence Errors questions, Improving Sentences questions ask you to spot *and* correct the errors.

22. Jean-Marie <u>planning</u> to go to college next fall.

   (A) planning
   (B) are planning
   (C) have planned
   (D) with a plan
   (E) plans

The problem here is tense. "Jean-Marie planning" is incorrect. Choice (E) clearly and concisely uses the proper tense in the context of the sentence.

Right off the bat, you should notice there are a few differences between Improving Sentences and Identifying Sentence Errors.

What's different? First, there's more work to do. Not only do you have to spot an error but you will now also have to correct it. As you read in the instructions, you must correct the sentence without changing its meaning—"clear and precise, without awkwardness and ambiguity." A lovely sentiment, right?

The other thing that's different? If you decide that the sentence is correct as written, the answer is now (A). Answer choice (A) repeats the underlined portion of the sentence exactly as it was originally written. Which brings us to what is **the same** about these two sections:

Not all Improving Sentences questions have an error.

In approximately one-fifth of the Improving Sentences questions, the answer will be (A), no error.

Sound familiar? It should. Just as in Identifying Sentence Errors, keep an eye out for sentences that are correct as written. Don't go crazy looking for something to be wrong.

PROCESS OF ELIMINATION

When the people at ETS came up with the notion of questions in the Improving Sentences format, what do you suppose they thought most students would do? We like to imagine that they hoped students would sit there and read every sentence five times over with each answer choice substituted for the underlined section. Imagine their glee at discovering a question type that would slow almost everyone down.

EXCEPT YOU.

FIND THE ERROR FIRST

In many ways, your first step in Improving Sentences will be just like your first and final steps in Identifying Sentences Errors. When you read the sentence, first try to decide what could be wrong with it. Think of some of the items from the checklist. Is there an opening modifier? Are there pronouns? Do subject and verb agree? Are there any comparisons, idiomatic phrases, and so on? If you spot the error, your first step is complete.

Then, eliminate (A) and *any choice that repeats the error.*

Be aggressive: Identify the error *before* you go to the answer choices.

AGGRESSIVENESS DRILL

See if you can find the error, if one exists, without answer choices to refer to. Circle the mistake in the underlined part of the sentence. Correct the sentence if you can.

1. When you begin a new exercise routine, <u>they can expect to feel better as well as lose weight.</u>

    _____

    _____

2. <u>If I was any faster, I would be winning every race I run.</u>

    _____

    _____

3. The house down the street is <u>not as pretty as Mrs. Jones.</u>

    _____

    _____

4. The librarian asked Marie to tell her <u>which book she wanted.</u>

    _____

    _____

5. Yesterday I lay in the sun all day, and now I have a terrible sunburn.

_____

_____

6. Marie felt that the class wasn't scarcely tolerable at all.

_____

_____

7. When you take your pet to the veterinarian, make sure they have a leash.

_____

_____

8. I have been working on this project for such a long period of time that I'm beginning to hate it.

_____

_____

9. Cathy and Derek decided that the story about which they were writing was stupid.

_____

_____

10. Neither of my sisters want to go with me to the movies.

_____

_____

Answers are on page 96.

Eliminate any answer choice that repeats the error.

I'VE SPOTTED THE ERROR—NOW WHAT?

At this point, even if you can't decide which of the remaining choices is correct, you will still guess. Remember our BIG IMPORTANT RULE?

ANYTIME YOU CAN ELIMINATE EVEN
ONE WRONG ANSWER CHOICE, YOU MUST GUESS.

But before you jump at that guess, take a look at the answer choices. With luck, you have eliminated at least two choices by spotting the error in the sentence and crossing out any choice that repeats that error. Now, think like an ETS question writer. The way to construct wrong answers is typically to correct the original mistake and make new mistakes on the remaining choices. Knock out any new mistakes and choices that change the meaning of the original sentence.

Keep in mind a couple of hints

Hint 1:

Avoid "-ing" words. This type of construction is almost always awkward and therefore, to ETS, incorrect. "-ing" words aren't wrong by definition, but be very sure if you pick an answer choice with an "-ing" word that there isn't a better choice.

Be wary of *-ing* words such as *being*.

Look at the following example:

Being the best in her class at math and science, Barbie is considered a shoo-in for the award.

(A) Being the best in her class at math and science
(B) Being the best in her class for math and science as well
(C) By being the best in her class for math and science
(D) With her best command of math and science
(E) Because she is the best in her class at math and science

(A), (B), and (C) all have the same awkward "-ing" construction. Eliminate them and you're left with (D) and (E). Since (D) uses a strange prepositional phrase that slightly changes the meaning of the sentence, (E) is the clear winner.

Hint 2:

Look to the shortest answers.

Remember that good English is generally concise and clear. Often, sentences go astray with lots of extra words. This is not an ironclad rule, of course, but short answers are good places to look and good guesses if you have narrowed your choices to two and *can't imagine* why one choice would be better than the other.

Concise answer choices tend to be good guesses.

SECTION AND QUESTION ORDER

Do the Improving Sentences questions last. They are a little more time-consuming than Identifying Sentence Errors, but slightly more intimidating than Improving Paragraphs.

As far as question order goes, the same holds true as for Identifying Sentence Errors. There is no real order of difficulty, so don't hesitate to skip a few questions on your first pass. You will probably have time to come back to them later, and if you don't, then you just skipped the ones you were less likely to answer correctly.

FINAL IMPROVING SENTENCES WRAP-UP

- Look for the error *before* you look at the answer choices. Eliminate all choices that repeat the original error.

- Using your checklist, scan for errors among the remaining choices.

- Avoid answer choices that contain "-ing" words.

- When in doubt, go with shorter choices.

- DON'T FORGET—approximately one-fifth of the Improving Sentences will be (A), no error.

> Use a two-pass system on the Improving Sentences questions. Do the easy ones first and then go back to the hard ones.

IMPROVING SENTENCES DRILL

Circle the best answer choice.

 1. After having worked so long on the project, receiving a C was very disheartening to Christina.

    (A) receiving a C was very disheartening to Christina
    (B) the grade of C was very disheartening to Christina
    (C) disheartened at a C was Christina
    (D) Christina was very disheartened to receive a C
    (E) Christina's receiving of a C was very disheartening

2. In a library, materials are stored for a purpose that is as often retrieval as it is for information.

    (A) that is as often retrieval as it is for information
    (B) that is as often to retrieve as it is to inform
    (C) that is as often for retrieval as for informing
    (D) that is as often retrieving as informing
    (E) that often is for retrieval as for information

3. We should be more interested in gathering pertinent data on the candidate <u>not what he looks like on a television show</u>.

   (A) not what he looks like on a television show
   (B) as in his appearance on a television show
   (C) than about an appearance on a television show
   (D) than the appearance of the candidate on a television show
   (E) than in his appearance on television shows

4. Long dismissed as noxious, unprofitable places, wetlands <u>are now prized as some of the richest ecosystems on earth</u>.

   (A) are now prized as some of the richest ecosystems on earth
   (B) are now the most prized of rich ecosystems of the earth
   (C) is now prized as one of the richest ecosystems on earth
   (D) are now prized as the richer of the earth's ecosystems.
   (E) is prized now as one of the richest of the world ecosystems

5. Billed as "Tiger of the Human Race," <u>a small fortune was made by Geronimo while he was a prisoner</u>.

   (A) a small fortune was made by Geronimo while he was a prisoner
   (B) while he was a prisoner Geronimo made a small fortune
   (C) Geronimo made a small fortune while he was a prisoner
   (D) Geronimo, a small fortune made, was a prisoner
   (E) while kept prisoner, Geronimo made a small fortune

6. From a skin boat, <u>harpoons a bowhead whale on St. Lawrence Island</u>.

   (A) harpoons a bowhead whale on St. Lawrence Island
   (B) on St. Lawrence Island, harpoons a bowhead whale
   (C) on St. Lawrence Island, harpooning a bowhead whale
   (D) a bowhead whale is harpooned on St. Lawrence Island
   (E) whalers harpoon a bowhead whale on St. Lawrence Island

E   7.   The Japanese have developed a computerized
         cleaner that <u>vacuums, dusts, and is working
         underwater</u>.

         (A) vacuums, dusts, and is working underwater
         (B) vacuums, dusts, and underwater will work
         (C) vacuums, will dust, and will work underwater
         (D) will vacuum, will dust, and underwater works
         (E) vacuums, dusts, and works underwater

    8.   <u>Whether my mother really told me to wash the car
         or did not</u> remains a mystery, but that I will get
         punished is certain.

         (A) Whether my mother really told me to wash the
              car or did not
         (B) Whether in truth my mother told me to wash
              the car or did not tell me so
         (C) The reality of whether my mother asked me to
              wash the car or not
         (D) Whether my mother really told me to wash
              the car
         (E) That my mother really might have told me to
              wash the car

    9.   Food production has decreased, even though <u>the
         number of people needing to be fed has increased</u>.

         (A) the number of people needing to be fed has
              increased
         (B) the number of people needing food has
              increasing
         (C) the amount of people needing to be fed has
              increased
         (D) the amount of people needing food is
              increasing
         (E) there is an increasing number of people since
              then which need food

    10. Although Tama Janowitz and Jay McInerney both
         have new books on the market, <u>only one of the two
         are successful</u>.

         (A) only one of the two are successful
         (B) only one of the two is successful
         (C) only one of the two books are successful
         (D) only one of the two books is successful
         (E) one only of the books has been successfully

    11. Boys generally have higher test scores <u>than girls,
         but even though they have better grades in school</u>.

         (A) than girls, but even though they have better
              grades in school
         (B) but girls have better grades in school
         (C) than girls, but they still have better grades in
              school
         (D) than girls, but they have better grades in school
         (E) even though girls having the best grades in
              school

12. Many citizens objected to the government's new proclamation that gives candidates discretionary power to determine <u>about disclosing from where</u> they received funds.

(A) about disclosing from where
(B) whether he or she should be disclosing where
(C) if he or she should disclose where
(D) whether to disclose from where
(E) the disclosing of sources from which they received funds

13. Although Pierre is editor of the school paper, <u>he does not know the rules of grammar and has never written an article</u>.

(A) he does not know the rules of grammar and has never written an article
(B) it is without knowing the rules of grammar or writing an article
(C) he does not know the rules of grammar nor has written an article
(D) he does not know the rules of grammar and has never written one
(E) it is without the benefit of grammar or writing

14. <u>One of the more satisfying of the ten dishes offered by that restaurant are falafel</u>, a tasty chickpea burger.

(A) One of the more satisfying of the ten dishes offered by that restaurant are falafel
(B) One of the more satisfying of the ten dishes offered by that restaurant is falafel
(C) Falafel, one of the more satisfying of the ten dishes offered by that restaurant, is
(D) One of the most satisfying of the ten dishes offered by that restaurant is falafel
(E) One of the most satisfying of the restaurant's ten dishes are called falafel

15. The primary reasons given for the country's economic woe <u>is that they have poor leadership and a huge deficit</u>.

(A) is that they have poor leadership and a huge deficit
(B) are poor leadership ability and they have a huge deficit
(C) are poor leadership and a huge deficit
(D) is having poor leadership and having a huge deficit
(E) are poor leadership, in addition to a huge deficit

Answers are on pages 96-97.

7

Improving Paragraphs

There will be twelve Improving Paragraphs questions on the test. There will be two or three essays, each with approximately four to six questions. Read the instructions, so that you can get an idea of what you'll have to do.

Directions: Each of the following passages in an early draft of a student essay. Some parts of the passages need to be rewritten. Read each passage and select the best answers for the questions that follow. Some questions are about particular sentences or parts of sentences and ask you to improve sentence structure and word choice. Other questions refer to parts of the essay or the entire essay and ask you to consider organization and development. In making your decisions, follow the conventions of standard written English. After you have chosen your answer, fill in the corresponding oval on your answer sheet.

WHAT'S DIFFERENT ABOUT IMPROVING PARAGRAPHS?

First of all, you are not necessarily looking for errors. The short essay is intended to look like a first draft, and you will need to make revisions to it. There may be some grammatical errors, but more likely you will be asked to make an awkward construction more clear or less awkward. In general, you will be asked to do one of three things:

> *Improving Paragraphs questions usually ask you to make an awkward construction more clear or less awkward. These questions don't have to ask you about grammar.*

1. Revise a sentence.
    Make sure you read the question carefully. You will be asked to revise either just an underlined portion of the sentence, or the whole sentence.

2. Combine sentences.
    You will have to combine two or three sentences into one well-written sentence.

3. Answer general questions about the organization of the passage. You may be asked to add a sentence, move a sentence, or identify how a sentence works.

> *There are three types of Improving Paragraphs questions: revising a sentence, combining sentences, and general questions.*

Look at each type of question and go through some general ways to handle each.

BEFORE YOU IMPROVE ANYTHING...

Give the passage a quick read through. Don't waste time looking for errors or awkward construction. Take a minute to see what the essay is about before you begin to tackle questions about specific parts. It is helpful to know the subject. *Don't* spend more than one minute doing this.

HOW TO REVISE A SENTENCE

First of all, read the question carefully. You may be asked to revise only a part of the sentence. If so, the part you need to revise will be underlined. You may be asked to revise the whole sentence. Take a look at this example.

Another was because she was the first woman hired by
the firm.

The answer choices here will contain possible ways to revise that sentence. Now, remember, this sentence is just part of an essay, so whenever you do an Improving Paragraphs question, don't lose sight of the fact that you are being asked to revise in context. Remember the following:

> Read the sentences before and after the sentence you are revising.

Frequently, these sentences will help you understand the best way to revise the sentence in the question.

Here, the sentence before read:

> One reason that Jane received so much criticism from her fellow workers was that she was so young.

Now look at the two together, only this time, fill in the underlined portion of the sentence yourself and see if you come up with an answer similar to the choices you're given.

> One reason that Jane received so much criticism from her fellow workers was that she was so young. Another _____ the first woman hired by the firm.

Now look at the answers:

(A) was that which she was
(B) reason was that she was
(C) comes from that she was
(D) reason was due to the circumstance that she was
(E) was caused by the fact that she was being

Did you come up with a version that was close to the correct answer (B)? Notice that the structure in the sentence to be revised is now like the structure in the sentence that preceded it. That sentence read "One reason was that . . ." and the revised sentence now reads "Another reason was that. . . ." Remember not to be afraid to make the sentences sound simple. A well-written sentence is often short and sweet. Before we do any more, let's summarize the three rules for sentence revision:

◆ Read the directions carefully. Are you asked to revise the whole sentence or only a portion of it?

◆ Read the sentences *around* the sentence you are revising. They will usually give you a clue about a good way to structure the sentence in the question.

Don't just read the sentence that needs revision. Read the surrounding sentences as well.

- Try to rewrite the sentence, or underlined portion of the sentence in your head before going to the answer choices. If you see something like your version, go with it. If not, look for the answer that comes closest in form to the surrounding sentences. Stay away from long, convoluted answers. Correct English is often concise as well as clear.

Remember to always start eliminating choices as soon as you can. If you don't see your answer right away, start crossing out those that you know are incorrect. Zero in on the choices that may be correct and look at each critically. Looking for what is wrong with an answer is frequently easier than finding what is right about it.

Keep in mind:

- Avoid "-ing" verbs

- Avoid ambiguity

- Look for differences among the remaining choices

SENTENCE REVISION DRILL

Try your hand at rewriting the following underlined sentences or sentence parts. Sometimes another sentence is given to show you the context. Remember that there's no exact right answer, but see if your sentence is similar to the one in the answer key on page 97.

1. One way to meet people is to go to parties. <u>Also to go to meetings or extracurricular activities.</u>

   Another way is to go to ...

2. In the modern world there are many stresses on the family <u>and mainly this is because of all the complex problems in the world that are to blame.</u>

   caused by the c p in the w

3. If you want to go to law school you'll need to do well on the LSAT. <u>To have good grades is important.</u>

   You'll need good grades also

4. Orville and Wilbur Wright were the first to make a powered, controlled, <u>and also sustained as well</u> <u>airplane flight</u>.

_____

_____

5. You need oxygen to live. <u>Get it by breathing air</u> <u>that contains oxygen.</u>

_____

_____

HOW TO COMBINE SENTENCES

You will also be asked to combine two or three sentences into one. If you handle these carefully, you should be whipping through them in no time. Here, read only the sentences you need to combine. It is not necessary to understand their context. You are simply being tested on your ability to combine sentences without getting awkward.

- ◆ Try covering the answers and writing the sentence in your head first. As with all these types of questions, the answers frequently throw you off. Have an idea of where you'd like to go before you go to the choices and you won't be so easily led astray.

- ◆ Remember that combining usually tests your use of commas and conjunctions. If you're not sure about when to use a comma, a semicolon, or a colon, refer to the explanations below.

> Read only the sentences you need to combine. Try to combine the sentences yourself *before* you go to the answer choices.

THE PRINCETON REVIEW PUNCTUATION CHART

Commas

Commas are used for about a thousand different things, but when joining sentences, you need only remember that a comma is used with a conjunction (and, but, or, etc.).
Example: *I went to the store, but I couldn't find what I wanted.*

Semicolons

Use the semicolon whenever you don't use the conjunction. A fairly reliable rule of thumb is that if the two parts sound fine as separate sentences, then they have a semicolon between them.
Example: *I went to the store; there, I found the CD I wanted.*

> Combining sentences often involves the use of commas, semicolons, and colons.

Colons

The colon is as close to a period as you get in punctuation land. It also can be used to set off an example or list.
Example: *I've always said: "Shop at that store if you need a CD!"* or, *A CD: the perfect gift!*

Don't use too many "ands"—you will end up with a run-on sentence. A run-on sentence is one of the most common errors made when combining more than two sentences.

Go with the flow. In other words, take a look at the sentences you are combining. Are they basically the same in tone and intent? Do they switch gears? Decide beforehand which conjunction would make sense.

CONJUNCTIONS THAT GO WITH THE FLOW
CONJUNCTIONS THAT GO AGAINST THE FLOW

With	Against
and	although
so	but
; (semicolon)	however
, (comma)	nevertheless
— (dash)	nonetheless
: (colon)	negative words like "unfortunately"

Watch out for misplaced modifiers. Whenever you combine sentences, be careful to avoid ambiguity. Putting the wrong modifier next to the wrong sentence will make the sentences unclear.

Look at the following three sentences:

> *"Juan and Pierre have promising careers."*

> *"Juan intends to be a veterinarian."*

> *"Pierre would like to be a writer."*

And an incorrect choice:

> *"Juan and Pierre have promising careers as a veterinarian and a writer."*

Who's the vet and who's the writer?
How about:

> *"Juan and Pierre have promising careers: Juan as a veterinarian and Pierre as a writer."*

Let's sum up sentence combining:

- ◆ Try writing the new sentence in your head first.
- ◆ Combining usually tests punctuation and conjunctions.
- ◆ Don't use too many "ands."
- ◆ Go with the flow. Use the right type of conjunction.
- ◆ Watch out for misplaced modifiers.

COMBINING SENTENCES DRILL

Combine the sentences in each example into one. Your version may not match the one on page 97 exactly, but it should come close. Did you use the right punctuation and conjunction?

1. Paul wants to bring lunch to the game tomorrow. David prefers to buy lunch there.

   _____

   _____

2. Some people like to work long hours to earn extra money. Others prefer to look for better-paying jobs.

   _____

   _____

3. One of the great features of E-mail is that you can send messages instantly. The other is that you can receive messages instantly.

   _____

   _____

4. I used to like to go shopping. Now, I find it to be more a chore than anything. The malls are so crowded.

   _____

   _____

5. Desktop publishing is the latest thing. Did you know that there's a conference about it next month? It's at the high school in town.

   _____

   _____

6. Gliders can be launched in a variety of ways. They can be pulled by cable. They can be launched with a powerful winch.

   _____

   _____

Answers are on page 97.

How to Answer General Questions

Save general questions for last.

- ◆ Always do these last! You may be able to answer them without any further reading. After reading through all the specific questions, you will often find that you have all the information you need.

- ◆ Once again, read the question carefully. If you need to read more, check to see what exactly you need to read. Does the question ask about the information in paragraph three only?

- ◆ Look for key words in the passage.

Compare the following:

The question:

> Why does the author mention the car in paragraph three?

The sentence it refers to:

> *The car serves as a perfect example of this theory.*

The correct answer:

> (C) To provide an example.

- ◆ You may be asked to add a sentence to improve the continuity of the passage. Remember your flow words.

IMPROVING PARAGRAPHS DRILL

Try your hand at the following questions. Remember the directions, and read the tips. Answers are on page 97.

Questions 1-6 are based on the following passage.

(1) Conservation and ecology are the hot topics at out school. (2) Students used to just throw everything out in the one big garbage pail. (3) Sure, it was easy. (4) It wasn't good for the environment.

(5) I volunteered to head up the conservation team. (6) My friends and I decided to map out our strategies. (7) First we needed to get students to become aware of the problem. (8) Educating was important. (9) A thing to do was to implement a recycling program. (10) We checked with the local town government. (11) They would supply the recycling bins. (12) We had to supply the people who'd be willing to recycle. (13) The most important thing students had to learn to do was to separate their garbage. (14) Glass in one container. (15) Plastic in another.

(16) Our final step was to get the teachers and administrators involved. (17) Paper can be recycled too. (18) We ran a poster contest. (19) The winners are hanging in our halls. (20) Reuse, recycle, renew. (21) That's our school's motto.

1. Which of the following represents the best way to combine sentences 3 and 4 (reproduced below)?

    Sure it was easy. It wasn't good for the environment.

    (A) Sure, it was easy and not good for the environment either.
    (B) Even though it was not good for the environment it was not easy.
    (C) Sure, it was easy, but it wasn't good for the environment.
    (D) It was easy although surely not good for the environment either.
    (E) Sure it was easy; not good for the environment.

2. Which of the following sentences, if added after sentence 4, would best serve to link the first paragraph to the second paragraph?

    (A) Unfortunately, the environment suffered.
    (B) We needed to make a change.
    (C) Easy things are often not good for the environment.
    (D) However, people can be very lazy.
    (E) The school was against any change.

3. Which of the following represents the best revision of the underlined portions of sentences 7 and 8 (reproduced below)?

First we needed to get students to become aware of the problem. Educating was important.

(A) problem for educating was important.
(B) problem of educating. It was important.
(C) problem to educate was important.
(D) problem: education was important.
(E) problem for education was important to us.

4. In the context of the second paragraph, what is the best way to revise sentence 9?

(A) Next, we needed to implement a recycling program.
(B) Implementing a recycling program was a thing to do.
(C) A recycling program needed to be implemented.
(D) Implementing a program for recycling was the step that would be next.
(E) A program would need to be implemented next for recycling.

5. In relation to the passage as a whole, which of the following best describes the writer's intention in the second paragraph?

(A) To show cause and effect.
(B) To give an example.
(C) To explain a solution to a problem.
(D) To evaluate a proposal.
(E) To contradict an opinion set out in the first paragraph.

6. Which of the following represents the most effective way to combine sentences 20 and 21 (reproduced below)?

Reuse, recycle, renew. That's our school's new motto.

(A) Reuse, recycle, renew and you know our school's motto.
(B) The motto of our school is that: Reuse, recycle, renew.
(C) Reuse, recycle, renew are the motto of our school now.
(D) The motto of our school is reusing, recycling, and renewing.
(E) Reuse, recycle, renew is now our school's motto.

Questions 7-12 are based on the following passage.

(1) Whenever you visit a city, take a look at the skyscrapers. (2) They often form the skyline in big cities. (3) They give each one a distinct personality. (4) It's interesting to look at them and imagine how they were built. (5) Not at all like houses.

(6) In a house, the walls support the floors and roof. (7) Not so in a skyscraper. (8) The walls couldn't do that. (9) It's all too heavy. (10) There's a frame there that does that. (11) Frames are made of steel or concrete. (12) Sometimes these parts are made someplace else. (13) Then they need to bring them there and put them on the building.

(14) I guess everyone knows that the tallest building in the world is the Sears Tower. (15) It's in Chicago. (16) It's 1,454 feet tall. (17) That's a lot of concrete and steel.

7. Which of the following represents the best way to combine sentences 2 and 3 (reproduced below)?

They often form the skyline in big cities. They give each one a distinct personality.

(A) They often form the skyline in big cities, giving each a distinct personality.
(B) Each with its own personality forms a skyline in big cities.
(C) A distinct personality is formed in the skyline by each.
(D) They often form skylines and distinct personalities.
(E) In each, they form skylines and personalities for cities.

8. Which of the following represents the best way to revise the underlined portions of sentences 4 and 5 (reproduced below)?

It's interesting to look at them and imagine how they were built. They're not at all like houses.

(A) built, but not at all like houses.
(B) built not like houses.
(C) built, however, not at all like houses.
(D) built: not at all like the house.
(E) built, for the skyscraper is not built as houses are.

9. Which of the following represents the best way to combine sentences 7, 8, and 9 (reproduced below)?

   Not so in a skyscraper. The walls couldn't do that. It's all too heavy.

   (A) Not so in a skyscraper because the walls can't do that, they're too heavy.
   (B) The walls couldn't do that because it's all too heavy in a skyscraper.
   (C) In a skyscraper, that's not so because it's all too heavy.
   (D) In a skyscraper, the walls couldn't support the structure because the skyscraper is too heavy.
   (E) The walls couldn't do that: it's all too heavy in a skyscraper.

10. Which of the following represents the best revision of sentence 10?

   (A) There's a frame there doing that.
   (B) In a skyscraper, a frame supports the floors and roof.
   (C) A frame does that there.
   (D) There's a frame in the skyscraper doing that.
   (E) A frame there in the skyscraper does that there.

11. In relation to the passage as a whole, which of the following describes the function of the last paragraph?

   (A) To support the theory in the second paragraph.
   (B) To contradict the main idea of the passage.
   (C) To give an example.
   (D) To distract the reader from the ideas in the second paragraph.
   (E) To evaluate the data in the second paragraph.

12. Which of the following represents the best way to combine sentences 15 and 16 (reproduced below)?

   It's in Chicago. It's 1,454 feet tall.

   (A) It's in Chicago, but it's 1,454 feet tall.
   (B) It's in Chicago, and it's 1,454 feet tall.
   (C) In Chicago, it is 1,454 feet tall as well.
   (D) It's 1,454 feet tall in Chicago.
   (E) In Chicago, 1,454 feet tall it is.

8

The Essay

This chapter is all about getting you to write an essay that will get a good score *on the SAT II: Writing Test.* It is not about writing essays for, say, your college applications or your English class; someone will probably read *those* carefully.

On the SAT II: Writing Test, you needn't worry about that. Check out these directions:

You have 20 minutes to write an essay on the topic assigned below. DO NOT WRITE ON ANOTHER TOPIC. AN ESSAY ON ANOTHER TOPIC IS NOT ACCEPTABLE.

The essay is assigned to give you an opportunity to show how well you can write. You should, therefore, take care to express your thoughts on the topic clearly and effectively. How well you write is much more important than how much you write, but to cover the topic adequately you will probably need to write more than one paragraph. Be specific.

Your essay must be written on the lines provided on your answer sheet. You will receive no other paper on which to write. You will find that you have enough space if you write on every line, avoid wide margins, and keep your handwriting to a reasonable size. It is important to remember that what you write will be read be someone who is not familiar with your handwriting. Try to write or print so that what you are writing is legible to the reader.

Consider carefully the following quotation and the assignment below it. Then plan and write your essay as directed.

"History repeats itself."

Assignment: Choose a specific example from personal experience, current events, or from your reading in history, literature, or other subjects and use this example as the basis for an essay in which you agree or disagree with the statement above. Be sure to be specific.

WHEN THE SUPERVISOR ANNOUNCES THAT TWENTY MINUTES HAVE PASSED, YOU MUST STOP WRITING THE ESSAY AND GO ON TO PART B IF YOU HAVE NOT ALREADY DONE SO. IF YOU FINISH YOUR ESSAY BEFORE THIS ANNOUNCEMENT, GO ON TO PART B AT ONCE.

YOU MAY MAKE NOTES ON THIS PAGE AND ON THE OPPOSITE PAGE BUT YOU MUST WRITE YOUR ESSAY ON THE ANSWER SHEET.

Apparently, handwriting is very important to these people. It would be to you as well.

You see, to grade the writing sample, ETS manages to round up 150 desperate high school and college English teachers. During this time, the *92,000* or so essays written will each be graded by two separate people. That's *184,000* readings by *150* people in one week. Can you imagine how annoying it is if the essays are messy?

ETS says the essay is graded *holistically.* That means they look at the total *impression* that the essay gives. In about two minutes, what kind of impression can you make? Well, the good news is, a very good one, with a little practice.

How the Essay Is Scored

The multiple-choice part of the test is worth 600 points; the essay is worth 200.

Your essay is read by two people. Each will give the essay a score on a scale of 1 to 6, 6 being the highest. The two scores are added together and translate into the following contributions to your total score:

The essay, which is graded by two people, is scored on a scale of 1 to 6 (low to high).

TOTAL SCORE	CONTRIBUTION
2	0
3	20
4	40
5	60
6	80
7	100
8	120
9	140
10	160
11	180
12	200

What ETS Says Is Graded

ETS publications tell you that graders are encouraged to look at what has been done well, rather than what hasn't been done. Obviously, careful scrutiny is just not possible.

The essay score is converted from the 1-to-6 scale to a 0-to-200 scale.

What Does This Mean?

It means that one or two misspellings probably won't hurt your score. It means that a mispunctuation or missing apostrophe is not cause for alarm.

What you're creating is a good impression. Although we're not advocating carelessness, little mistakes are not a big deal in the graders' eyes. What apparently impresses graders is length. In fact, if you checked out what ETS considers to be the paradigms of a great essay and a bad essay, it becomes overwhelmingly clear that one thing is valued more than any other:

Length

You see, *holistically*, this screams out, "I have something to say; I have thought it out; I am relating it fully to you."

Some Additional Pointers

- **Fill as many lines as possible.**

  As we said before, more is better. You get forty-four lines to fill. Using forty-one is fine; using twenty is not. By the way, you cannot use more than the space you are given.

For the Writing Test, a good essay is a long one.

◆ **Indent, Indent, Indent.**

Your essay should be four or five paragraphs. Indentations say, "I'm organized and I know how to structure an essay."

◆ **Cite examples from history and literature.**

Can you imagine how much an *English* teacher will love you if you actually start talking about *Romeo and Juliet* to explain the sorrow of love lost, instead of your boyfriend or girlfriend? This can mean **big points**. Make sure, if you do cite any literary examples, to underline them. "Holistically," they will leap off the page. You should get some literary examples ready before the test begins so you won't have to sweat them the day of the exam.

◆ **A few big words are nice.**

Don't go crazy here. A few well-placed words, especially in the introduction or conclusion, will sure look nice. Words like *advocate, hypothetically, inevitable, allusion, objective, subjective.* If you have a copy of The Princeton Review's *Word Smart*, check it out. There are some beautiful big words there. Do not, however, use words that you are not comfortable with. Short words are better than misused words.

◆ **Simple is better than complex.**

Please don't let all this "long is better" stuff mislead you. Even though you'll be going for a longer essay, long sentences get convoluted quickly. And there's nothing like a little convolution to make an overworked English teacher cry. Keep sentences short and simple.

SOME SAMPLE ESSAYS

Let's take a look at a couple of sample essays written on the topic, " 'Tis better to have loved and lost than never to have loved at all."

Give yourself two minutes to read each essay. Take a second to jot down the good and bad points of each. Think about what sort of things you didn't notice and what sort of things you noticed right away.

Essay Number One

I agree with the statement " 'Tis better to have loved and lost than never to have loved at all." A life filled with love is most certainly better than a life without love. You cannot always worry about whether or not you will lose the love you work hard for.

In all aspects of life, whether it is sports, personal relationships, or study, you should work hard to be the best. You should always strive for "love" and not be concerned about losing. As in sports, when it is better to try really hard and get a home run sometimes than to only be mediocre and get a single.

    In personal relationships as well, you can't be afraid of losing your love. Just having had a wonderful experience, whether in personal relationships, or outside of them is worth the pain of loss.

Analysis

How was the essay presented?

_____

Any literary allusions?

_____

Overall, "holistic" impression?

_____

Your score (on a scale of 1–6) _____

    This essay would probably have received a score of 6 (each reader awarding 3 points out of a possible 6). It was competent, but not really well presented. It could have used better examples of why the author agreed with the topic. It's not very long, and therefore, in the mind of the grader, not very well developed.

Essay Number Two

    I definitely agree " 'Tis better to have loved and lost than never to have loved at all." What would life be worth living if you have no love at all in it?

    I may be young, but even in family relationships, it is better to have them, even if they are painful, than to be without a family. I am sure that the same is true as you go through life. It is better to try to have relationships, even if they do not last than to have no relationships. This is why it is most certainly better to love than not to love.

Analysis

How was the essay presented?

_____

Any literary allusions?

_____

Overall, "holistic" impression?

_____

Your score (on a scale of 1–6) _____

This essay would probably have received a score of 4 (each reader giving the essay a score of 2). The author's ideas were not very well developed. The sentences are long and rambling. There are no solid examples to back up the ideas. It's also much too SHORT!

Essay Number Three

I most certainly agree with the thesis " 'Tis better to have loved and lost than never to have loved at all." Both history and literature are filled with examples of characters who strove for great passion, without fear of losing. These are the people who achieve the greatest heights. The results, often loss and pain, are certainly outweighed by the greatness experienced along the way. Certainly, love, whether of life, country, or another, is worth fighting for and worth the pain that so often accompanies it.

Shakespeare's _Romeo and Juliet_ is probably the greatest example of this idea. The passion felt by Romeo and Juliet, despite the obstacles laid out before them, made it clear that their love was more important than the inevitable fate that awaited them—death. I have no doubt that these two would have verified that a love like theirs, no matter how brief and tragic, was great. It was certainly greater than suffering a long life without a passionate love.

In history as well, we can certainly see many who believed that love of country, no matter what the consequence, was a far greater good than to have no allegiance. The great patriot Nathan Hale held his head high at his execution and proclaimed, "I only regret that I have but one life to give for my country." Had the great leaders of our revolution cared more about being safe, then about love of their ideals and of their country, we would never have won independence from English tyranny. It was men like Nathan Hale, who were willing to lose everything in the struggle for their great love—the love of country, who were responsible for the greatness of our country.

> *It is without a doubt that "'Tis better to have loved and lost than never to have loved at all." History, literature and life itself bear witness to that idea every day.*

Analysis

How was the essay presented?

_____

Any literary allusions?

_____

Overall, "holistic" impression?

_____

Your score (on a scale of 1–6) _____

This essay would probably have received a perfect score of 12 (a score of 6 from each grader). It's well presented and well written. Its main idea is supported by examples from literature and history. It's also nice and long. You may notice that there were a couple of minor errors ("then" instead of "than" near the end). But these don't really matter. As a whole, it is an impressive, thoughtful essay. A small error won't detract from the overall impression.

ESSAY DRILL

For each of the following quotations, think of three examples, either pro or con, or both, that you could use in an essay.

1. " 'Tis better to have loved and lost, than never to have loved at all."

	Pro		Con
1.	_____	1.	_____
2.	_____	2.	_____
3.	_____	3.	_____

2. "Neither a borrower nor a lender be."

	Pro		Con
1.	_____	1.	_____
2.	_____	2.	_____
3.	_____	3.	_____

3. "If at first you don't succeed, try, try again."

Pro   Con

1. _____   1. _____
2. _____   2. _____
3. _____   3. _____

4. "Good things come in small packages."

Pro   Con

1. _____   1. _____
2. _____   2. _____
3. _____   3. _____

5. "Give me liberty or give me death."

Pro   Con

1. _____   1. _____
2. _____   2. _____
3. _____   3. _____

6. "History repeats itself."

Pro   Con

1. _____   1. _____
2. _____   2. _____
3. _____   3. _____

MAKE AN OUTLINE

When you have thought of your examples, make a quick outline and write it in the margin of the section where the question is. This will help you to stay on track. It will also keep you indenting!

Before you start writing, brainstorm! Then make an outline.

If you don't know where to start with an outline, don't worry. Luckily for you, the outline you will use will be pretty standard. It will look like this:

I. Agree or disagree with the statement.

This paragraph will take up only a line or two. Simply state your opinion, and perhaps write a simple line about why you have this opinion—a "Many people throughout history have shown this to be true" kind of thing.

II.   Your best example—from history or literature, if possible

This paragraph will explain how your example supports your idea. Remember to underline the title, and mention the author and protagonist.

III.   Example #2 from history or literature, if possible

Same as above. See if you can dredge up some history from your American or European history class.

IV.   (Optional) Example #3 from literature, history, or personal

Here, you may throw in a personal example, but keep it to lessons your grandmother, coach, or minister taught you, as opposed to "what I learned hanging with a gang."

V.   Warm concluding statement

Don't waste too much space here. You should only have a few lines with which to wrap up. "And that's why I believe what I believe" will do just fine.

OUTLINE DRILL

Choose four of the examples given in the last drill and practice writing an outline. When you enter your examples, make sure they are ones about which you know some facts. If you mention a war, make sure you know which countries were allies, for example.

Writing the outline should only take a few minutes. Don't spend more than three minutes gathering your examples and writing your outline. More than that and you're running into precious writing time.

Essay #1

I.   _____

II.   _____

III.   _____

IV.   _____

V.   _____

Essay #2

I.   _____

II.   _____

III.   _____

IV.   _____

V.   _____

Your essay should have an introduction, three supporting paragraphs, and a conclusion.

Essay #3

   I.   _____

   II.   _____

   III.   _____

   IV.   _____

   V.   _____

Essay #4

   I.   _____

   II.   _____

   III.   _____

   IV.   _____

   V.   _____

SAMPLE ESSAY

Give yourself twenty minutes and see how you do on this essay topic. Go through the checklist at the end.

"The greatest griefs are those we cause ourselves."

_____

_____

_____

_____

_____

_____

_____

_____

_____

_____

_____

_____

_____

_____

_____

_____

_____

_____

_____

_____

_____

_____

CHECKLIST

- Historical or literary references?
- Fill most of the space?
- Neat, with few cross-outs?
- Indented?
- Four or five paragraphs?

If you've covered all the items on the checklist, then you've written a strong Writing Test essay.

9

The Final Word on the Writing Test

The Final Word Before the Diagnostic

Now go back and review the test-taking tips. Review again the beginning sections on cracking the test. After taking the diagnostic, review your performance and ask yourself where your study time could be best spent. Don't waste a lot of time on one or two little things that you've missed. Review the pacing chart regularly before your exam. Keep track of your goals. Often, you don't need to get that many more questions correct to get a really great score.

Ask Yourself

Did you run out of time?

If you ran out of time and didn't get to a few easy questions at the end of the test, you're not discriminating enough when it comes to skipping questions. Don't linger in any one place too long—one question is *never* worth five minutes of your time. KEEP IN MIND:

> 40 MINUTES for 60 QUESTIONS = ROUGHLY 40 SECONDS PER QUESTION

Did you get a lot of "easy" questions wrong?

Sometimes when you look back and review, you can't believe you got such easy questions wrong. Slow down. Did you read the question correctly the first time around? Did you pick the right answer, but circle an incorrect choice? Rushing is the major cause of avoidable errors.

Did you mismark answers on your answer sheet?

It's not at all uncommon to skip a question and then fill in all the subsequent answers one up on your answer sheet. It's a really good idea to fill in answers in blocks: in other words, work on one page in your booklet, then transfer the eight or nine answers to the answer sheet all at once. Then go back to your booklet and work on the next page.

Always circle the answer you choose and cross out answers you decide are wrong. If you want to go back later and recheck a particular answer, you will avoid doubling your work. Let's say, for example, you decided that the answer to question 6 was either (A) or (D). If you go back to it later, you won't waste time considering (B), (C), and (E) if you've already crossed them out.

Are you skipping around while taking the test?

Be a discriminating test taker! Look for a question that appeals to you and begin with that. If by any chance you see something that you recognize, you'll be a few steps ahead of the game—do that first.

Finally, Good Luck! You're Well Prepared!

Make sure to show up at the test site with lots of #2 pencils (with good erasers), a reliable watch, and a small snack to munch on in case you have to wait or if you're taking more than one test in a day. Remember, test results take six weeks to arrive, so when you're finished, go home, refuse to talk about it, and wait with supreme confidence for well-deserved great scores.

Don't forget about your pacing when taking the diagnostic test. You don't have to answer every question.

Remember to do easy questions first and then go back to the hard ones. Never get bogged down in one question.

Don't rush. This only results in careless errors.

Try bubbling in your answers a page at a time instead of a question at a time.

PART III

Answer Key to Drills

Grammar, Grammar, Grammar

Tense Drill, page 24

1. lie
2. lay
3. swam
4. had swum
5. stung
6. were
7. would have
8. would have spoken
9. rang
10. were

Subject-Verb Drill, page 26

1. is
2. is
3. is
4. is
5. are
6. knows
7. was
8. wants
9. is
10. is

Pronoun Agreement Drill, page 27

1. her
2. one
3. it
4. it is
5. they
6. he is
7. it's
8. it
9. she
10. their

Pronoun Case Drill, page 29

1. him
2. whom
3. she
4. my
5. whom
6. she
7. her
8. I
9. I
10. me

Idiom Drill, page 30

1. on
2. about
3. in
4. at
5. on
6. about
7. with
8. with
9. for
10. about

Parallelism Drill, page 31

1. submitted it to the teacher
2. skipping the sports
3. shopped for a new outfit
4. and no visitors after 12:00 A.M.
5. and compassionately
6. to learn good writing
7. and to do her homework before dinner
8. Calling the Screaming Blue Banshees
9. hiking, and
10. and scare

Noun Agreement Drill, page 32

1. "a member"— should be "members"
2. "his or her … restaurant"— should be "their … restaurants"
3. "a deal"—should be "deals"

4. "jar"—should be "jars"
5. "friend"—should be "friends"

Conjunction Drill, page 33

1. that
2. who is
3. which
4. but

Apples and Oranges Drill, page 34

1. than those of Monopoly
2. than do the people in the office next door
3. your dentist's technique
4. last year's (textbook)
5. than my mother's (cooking)
6. to your school's (team)
7. than cooking with meat
8. than his grade on the previous test
9. her friend's (dorm room)
10. just as her mother was

Misplaced Modifier Drill, pages 35-36

1. To pass English this year, all students must strictly adhere to the rules of grammar.
2. Even after applying a sunscreen with an SPF of 15, Sinead inevitably got a sunburn.
3. When Carla was six, her mother totaled the family car.
4. After returning to Kansas from her wild trip to Oz, poor old Dorothy found the farm boring.

5. Even though he was the best man for the job, Evan was overlooked by my boss.
6. To ensure the best possible protection, homeowners are urged to get life insurance policies.
7. Upon close inspection, he found that the diamond ring was a fake.
8. After taking her SAT II: Writing Subject Test, Gwen found that college was definitely in the picture.
9. Although he had never had much success at basketball, Paul scored the final point.

Word Choice Drill, page 38

1. prosecuted
2. incredible
3. eminent
4. allusions
5. fewer
6. accept

Redundancy Drill, page 39

The following pairs are the redundancies; either could be removed to correct the sentence.

1. the reason … because
2. A.M. … this morning
3. There's a good chance … probably
4. the year of (you have to say 1977, otherwise why would Gabrielle dance to the disco beat?)
5. consensus … of opinions
6. way … too (although way premature wouldn't really be right, eh?)

7. period ... of time

8. estimation ... approximate guess

9. I think ... in my opinion

Fragment Drill, page 40

1. He wants to come along. Or: Although he wants to come along, he can't.

2. I am going to the store to buy fruit.

3. I am buying CDs for the party.

4. My dream is to go to college for four years.

Double Negative Drill, page 41

1. We could scarcely see the movie from our seats.

2. I don't want any of that candy; I'm on a diet.

3. I had been there but two minutes before my mother called.

4. We had hardly any money left after buying the new U2 CD.

More/Most Drill, page 42

1. loudest
2. prettier
3. eldest
4. among
5. most

Adjective/Adverb Drill, page 42

1. quickly
2. good
3. easy
4. easily

Ambiguity Drill, page 43

1. he
2. he

3. he, which (which job was he referring to?), and his

4. his and him

5. he

Identifying Sentence Errors

Aggressiveness Drill, page 49

1. C
   The audience *was* able—subject-verb agreement

2. E

3. B
   It should read *"rapidly spreading"*—adverb/adjective problem

4. C
   The student who *expects*—subject-verb agreement

Identifying Sentence Errors Drill, pages 51-54

1. C
   one ... *is*—subject-verb agreement

2. D
   bobbing ... playing ... and *putting*—parallelism

3. E
   The *whom* is correct!

4. A
   between you and *me*—pronoun case

5. E
   "it was he who had set" is right!

6. A
   The placement of "while taking" makes it sound like the pencil was taking the test—misplaced modifier

7. B
   You need a subject here—"the boat rocked back and forth"—sentence fragment

8. D

   I was planning *to attend*—idiom

9. B

   had scarcely—double negative

10. A

    Station*e*ry is the stuff you write on—word choice

11. E

    "Tall*er* than I" is correct

12. C

    Abide *by* the rules set—idiom

13. D

    You can't say something is most perfect

14. E

    James and Alice <u>each</u> need *a lunch*—<u>each</u> separates Alice and James into individuals who each need a singular lunch

15. C

    about *my* getting the seats—pronoun case

16. D

    Everyone … *his or her* routine—pronoun agreement

17. B

    an announcement *that*—conjunction

18. B

    ten pages or *fewer*—word choice

19. E

20. A

    The conjunction "since" does not make sense here. If the *subordinate* conjunction "although" had been used, the sentence would be fine—sentence fragment

21. C

    "one" what? *a newspaper* would be clearer—ambiguous pronoun

22. D

    "*as you go* through high school" would be clearer—ambiguous

23. C

    than the *rules* of chess—apples and oranges

24. A

    Susie's ability *to supervise*—idiom

25. D

    neither … *nor*—idiom

Improving Sentences

Aggressiveness Drill, pages 57-58

1. *you* can expect to feel better as well as lose weight.
2. If I *were* any faster, I would be winning every race I ran.
3. not as pretty as *Mrs. Jones's.*
4. which book *Marie* wanted.
5. No error.
6. Marie felt that the class *was scarcely* tolerable.
7. make sure *it has* a leash.
8. for such a *long time* that I'm beginning to hate it.
9. No error.
10. *Neither* of my sisters *wants* to go with me to the movies.

Improving Sentences Drill, pages 60-63

1. D

   misplaced modifier

2. B

   parallel construction

3. E
   parallel construction
4. A
   no error
5. C
   misplaced modifier
6. E
   sentence fragment
7. E
   parallel construction
8. D
   parallel construction
9. A
   no error
10. D
    subject-verb agreement
11. B
    ambiguous pronoun
12. D
    idiom
13. A
    no error
14. D
    subject-verb agreement
15. C
    subject-verb agreement

Improving Paragraphs

Sentence Revision Drill, pages 68-69

1. Another way is to go to meetings or participate in extracurricular activities.
2. ; the complex problems in the world are to blame.
3. You'll also need good grades.
4. and sustained airplane flight.
5. You get it by breathing air that contains oxygen.

Combining Sentences Drill, page 71

1. Paul wants to bring lunch to the game tomorrow, but David prefers to buy it there.
2. Some people like to work long hours to earn extra money, while others prefer to look for better-paying jobs.
3. Two of the great features of E-mail are that you can send and receive messages instantly.
4. I used to like to go shopping, but now I find it to be more a chore than anything because the malls are so crowded.
5. Desktop publishing is the latest thing; there's a conference next month at the high school in town.
6. Gliders can be launched in a variety of ways: pulled by cable or launched with a powerful winch.

Improving Paragraphs Drill, pages 73-76

1. C
2. B
3. D
4. A
5. C
6. E
7. A
8. E
9. D
10. B
11. C
12. B

PART **IV**

The Princeton Review
SAT II: Writing Tests

WRITING
SUBJECT TEST

WRITING TEST

<table>
<tr><td>PART A</td><td style="text-align:center">Time—20 minutes
1 Question</td><td>ESSAY</td></tr>
</table>

You have 20 minutes to write an essay on the topic assigned below. DO NOT WRITE ON ANOTHER TOPIC. AN ESSAY ON ANOTHER TOPIC IS NOT ACCEPTABLE.

The essay is assigned to give you an opportunity to show how well you can write. You should, therefore, take care to express your thoughts on the topic clearly and effectively. How well you write is much more important than how much you write, but to cover the topic adequately, you will probably need to write more than one paragraph. Be specific.

Your essay must be written on the lines provided on your answer sheet. You will receive no other paper on which to write. You will find that you have enough space if you write on every line, avoid wide margins, and keep your handwriting to a reasonable size. It is important to remember that what you write will be read by somebody who is not familiar with your handwriting. Try to write or print so that what you are writing is legible to the reader.

Consider carefully the following quotation and the assignment below it. Then plan and write your essay as directed.

"It is better to give than to receive."

<u>Assignment</u>: Choose a specific example from personal experience, current events, or from your reading in history, literature, or other subjects and use this example as the basis for an essay in which you agree or disagree with the statement above. Be sure to be specific.

WHEN THE SUPERVISOR ANNOUNCES THAT TWENTY MINUTES HAVE PASSED, YOU MUST STOP WRITING THE ESSAY AND GO ON TO PART B IF YOU HAVE NOT ALREADY DONE SO. IF YOU FINISH YOUR ESSAY BEFORE THIS ANNOUNCEMENT, GO ON TO PART B AT ONCE.

YOU MAY MAKE NOTES ON THIS PAGE AND ON THE OPPOSITE PAGE BUT YOU MUST WRITE YOUR ESSAY ON THE ANSWER SHEET.

You may use this page to take notes as you plan your essay. Remember, however, that your essay MUST be written on the lined pages of the separate answer sheet.

PART B	Time—40 minutes 60 Questions	For each question in this part, select the best answer from among the choices given and fill in the corresponding oval on the answer sheet.

Directions: The following sentences test your knowledge of grammar, usage, word choice, and idiom.

> Some sentences are correct.
> No sentence contains more than one error.

You will find that the error, if there is one, is underlined and lettered. Elements of the sentence that are not underlined will not be changed. In choosing answers, follow the requirements of standard written English.

If there is an error, select the <u>one underlined part</u> that must be changed in order to make the sentence correct, and fill in the corresponding oval on your answer sheet.

If there is no error, fill in answer oval E.

EXAMPLE:

<u>The other</u> delegates and <u>him</u> <u>immediately</u>
   A   B   C

accepted the resolution <u>drafted by</u> the
                         D

neutral states. <u>No error</u>
            E

SAMPLE ANSWER
Ⓐ ● Ⓒ Ⓓ Ⓔ

1. The statistics released <u>by</u> the state department
               A
<u>makes</u> the economic situation look <u>bleaker</u>
 B   C
than it really <u>is</u>. <u>No error</u>
        D   E

2. The Eastern Arrernte people <u>of Northern Territory</u>
                          A
in Australia <u>share</u> memories in the age-old carvings
           B
<u>of</u> circles and tracks that once served as gathering
C
<u>places</u> for song and dance. <u>No error</u>
  D   E

3. Just last month, 92-year-old Fydor, two weeks
<u>after</u> the announcement <u>of elections</u> in Soviet
 A   B
Georgia, <u>has cast</u> his first vote <u>in</u> 70 years.
         C   D
<u>No error</u>
 E

4. Eating <u>less</u> fat is one good way to lose weight;
      A
<u>to start</u> an exercise program <u>that is</u> aerobic and
   B   C
consistent is <u>another</u>. <u>No error</u>
        D   E

GO ON TO THE NEXT PAGE

A 5. If you look at the prices <u>close</u>, the "economy
                                       A
size" <u>of</u> detergent <u>is</u> actually more expensive
       B   C
<u>than</u> the smaller trial sizes. <u>No error</u>
 D   E

B 6. Off the coast of Maine <u>lies</u> Monhegan Island,
D   A
 <u>an artists'</u> community <u>with no</u> modern
     B   C
conveniences, the only one <u>of a</u> kind in the
                       D
area. <u>No error</u>
       E

7. The report <u>issued</u> by the corporate presidents <u>is</u>
C   A   B
not only inaccurate <u>and</u> <u>poorly</u> presented.
               C   D
<u>No error</u>
  E

8. Japan performed <u>well</u> in the 1980s <u>because</u>
Clē   A   B
<u>they were</u> <u>able to export</u> the high-quality
  C   D
technology demanded by consumers. <u>No error</u>
                             E

9. <u>When</u> the student council announced <u>its</u> intention
D A   B
to elect a minority representative, neither the

principal <u>nor</u> the superintendent <u>were</u> willing to
      C   D
comment on the issue. <u>No error</u>
                  E

10. <u>Because she felt ill</u> the day of the trial, the defense
E A
B attorney <u>is</u> concerned <u>about</u> the quality of <u>her</u>
         B   C   D
legal argument. <u>No error</u>
              E

11. <u>Unnerved</u> by her near collision with a reckless
C A
driver, <u>my mother</u> convinced <u>my brother and I</u> to
       B   C
wear <u>seat belts</u>. <u>No error</u>
     D   E

12. Fingerprint matching, <u>aided by</u> a new breed of
B   A
computer, once again <u>provide</u> police <u>with</u> an
                B   C
integral and viable piece <u>of</u> information. <u>No error</u>
                  D   E

13. Although <u>tainted</u> by controversy, Mark
        A
Twain's *Huckleberry Finn* still <u>enjoys</u> a place
                            B
<u>among</u> the <u>great</u> works of American fiction.
  C   D
<u>No error</u>
  E

14. <u>Most</u> of the conveniences <u>without which</u> the
B A   B
American household could seemingly not exist

<u>were</u> available <u>even</u> fifty years ago. <u>No error</u>
 C   D   E

GO ON TO THE NEXT PAGE

15. <u>Distraught</u> at the notion <u>of moving</u> in with her
       A   B

    family, Marie <u>having been</u> self-sufficient for
                 C

    <u>many years</u>. <u>No error</u>
      D   E

16. The newly built arts center and the exhibition

    <u>of impressionist</u> art <u>on display</u> in the building
      A   B

    <u>was</u> funded <u>by private</u> endowment.
     C   D

    <u>No error</u>
      E

17. Skiing in Vermont, <u>unlike Colorado,</u> <u>is</u> usually
                 A   B

    <u>hampered</u> by <u>icy snow</u> conditions and crowded
      C   D

    slopes. <u>No error</u>
           E

18. Neither the editorial endorsement offered by

    the city's most influential newspaper <u>or</u> the
                               A

    dramatic speech <u>made</u> at the convention <u>was</u>
               B   C

    enough to <u>save the candidate's</u> bad reputation.
              D

    <u>No error</u>
      E

19. The way <u>in which</u> John <u>responds</u> to the new
          A   B

    treatment <u>will</u> be pivotal in the company's
           C

    decision <u>to market</u> the new formula. <u>No error</u>
          D   E

20. The college catalog clearly <u>stated</u> <u>that</u> a reading
                      A   B

    knowledge of French <u>was</u> necessary <u>in</u> the
                 C   D

    ability to participate in the class. <u>No error</u>
                                E

GO ON TO THE NEXT PAGE →

Directions: In each of the following sentences, some part or all of the sentence is underlined. Below each sentence you will find five ways of phrasing the underlined part. Select the answer that produces the most effective sentence, one that is clear and exact, without awkwardness or ambiguity, and fill in the corresponding oval on your answer sheet. In choosing answers, follow the requirements of standard written English. Choose the answer that best expresses the meaning of the original sentence.

Answer (A) is always the same as the underlined part. Choose answer (A) if you think the original sentence needs no revision.

EXAMPLE:

Laura Ingalls Wilder published her first book and she was sixty-five years old then.

(A) and she was sixty-five years old then
(B) when she was sixty-five years old
(C) being age sixty-five years old
(D) upon the reaching of sixty-five years
(E) at the time when she was sixty-five

SAMPLE ANSWER

Ⓐ ● Ⓒ Ⓓ Ⓔ

21. The majority of people in this country still do not vote despite major campaigns by celebrities to encourage them to do so.

(A) despite major campaigns by celebrities
(B) with major campaigns by celebrities
(C) however great the effort made by celebrities
(D) when even celebrities are making the effort
(E) even though major campaign by celebrities

22. After the flood of recent complaints, the school board voted against mandatory mathematics in all grades, and they thereby achieved their goal of relaxing requirements.

(A) and they thereby achieved their goal
(B) by which means they achieved their goal
(C) thereby achieving the board's goal
(D) achieving a goal the board had hoped to
(E) to which end they were able to achieve their goal

23. The two requirements put out by the architectural committee was to maintain a harmony with the natural settings in the area, and keeping the efficiency of the homes high.

(A) was to maintain a harmony with the natural settings in the area, and keeping the efficiency of the homes high
(B) were maintaining a harmony with the natural settings in the area, and to keep the efficiency of the homes high
(C) was to maintain a harmony with the natural settings in the area, and to keep the efficiency of the homes high
(D) were to maintain a harmony with the natural settings in the area, and to keep the efficiency of the homes high
(E) was maintaining a harmony with the natural settings in the area, and keeping the efficiency of the homes high

GO ON TO THE NEXT PAGE

24. His latest best-seller having been published, the author Stephen King became obsessed with getting some of the critical acclaim that had long eluded him.

    (A) His latest best-seller having been published
    (B) Having been the latest best-seller published
    (C) His best-seller, having been the latest published
    (D) When having had the latest best-seller published
    (E) Having published his latest best-seller

25. Anyone with a little ingenuity can make his or her own clothes, the difficulty being that the time involved is usually quite great.

    (A) clothes, the difficulty being that the time involved
    (B) clothes, unfortunately for most the time that can be involved
    (C) clothes; you may find, however, that the time involved
    (D) clothes, but the time involved
    (E) clothes; the difficultly being that in sewing clothes, the time involved

26. Successful entrepreneurship is often a result not only of creativity, but also of hard work.

    (A) often a result not only of creativity, but also of hard work
    (B) as often a result of not only creativity, but hard work as well
    (C) sometimes a result of creativity and also a factor of hard work
    (D) often a result of creativity as well as hard work too
    (E) often considered as much creativity as hard work

27. Artists can offer startling representations of the world but with their responsibility to elevate humanity.

    (A) but with their responsibility
    (B) with the responsibility
    (C) having also the responsibility
    (D) but ought also
    (E) their responsibility being as well

28. Using the desperate campaign tactics of lying, snooping, and negative ads as well, Smithers was soundly defeated by her opponent.

    (A) Using the desperate campaign tactics of lying, snooping, and negative ads as well
    (B) Because of her desperate tactics of lying, snooping, and using negative ads
    (C) Using the desperate tactics of lying, snooping, and negative ads
    (D) By using the desperate tactics of lying, snooping, as well as negative ads
    (E) With the desperate tactics of lying, snooping, as well as negative ads

29. David always has the best time if he is playing the game by the rules laid out by the manufacturer.

    (A) if he is playing
    (B) in playing
    (C) when playing
    (D) playing
    (E) because he is playing

GO ON TO THE NEXT PAGE

30. A well-organized person can go through the day efficiently, <u>wasting little time or they waste none at all</u>.

    (A) wasting little time or they waste none at all
    (B) wasting little or no time
    (C) wasting little time or wasting none at all
    (D) wasting either little time or none
    (E) either little or no time being wasted

31. After reading Mary Shelley's masterpiece *Frankenstein*, <u>I couldn't hardly believe</u> that she was only nineteen when she wrote it.

    (A) I couldn't hardly believe
    (B) I could hardly not believe
    (C) I could but hardly believe
    (D) I could hardly be believing
    (E) I could hardly believe

32. The results of the recent election for mayor <u>were different than what I had expected</u>.

    (A) were different than what I had expected
    (B) are different than what I had expected
    (C) are different than what results I was expecting
    (D) were different from what results I was expecting
    (E) were different from what I had expected

33. <u>Flamboyant even in death, stories of the excesses of the funeral of Emperor Khai Dinh circulated around Vietnam.</u>

    (A) Flamboyant even in death, stories of the excesses of the funeral of Emperor Khai Dinh circulated around Vietnam.
    (B) Flamboyant even in death, Emperor Khai Dinh's excesses even in his funeral were circulated around Vietnam.
    (C) Emperor Khai Dinh, flamboyant even in death, had excesses rumored by the people of Vietnam even in his funeral.
    (D) Stories of the excesses of the funeral of Emperor Khai Dinh, flamboyant even in death, circulated around Vietnam.
    (E) Circulated around Vietnam, Emperor Khai Dinh's funeral was rumored to be excessive.

34. Even though Paul has never even been on a pair of skis, <u>his room is decorated with skiing posters and he subscribes to skiing magazines</u>.

    (A) his room is decorated with skiing posters and he subscribes to skiing magazines
    (B) it is surprising to find his room decorated with skiing posters and that he subscribes to skiing magazines
    (C) his room is decorated with posters of them and he subscribes to magazines about them
    (D) his room is decorated with skiing posters and he subscribes to skiing magazines as well
    (E) he still decorates his room with skiing posters in addition to subscribing to skiing magazines

35. Historians claim that the German battleship *Bismarck*, <u>which was sunk in 1941 and lies three miles deep in the North Atlantic</u>, would be an important artifact if it were recovered.

    (A) which was sunk in 1941 and lies three miles deep in the North Atlantic
    (B) located three miles deep in the North Atlantic after being sunk in 1941
    (C) sunk in 1941 and lying in the North Atlantic three miles deep
    (D) being sunk in 1941 and lying three miles deep in the North Atlantic
    (E) after sinking in 1941, which lies three miles deep in the North Atlantic

GO ON TO THE NEXT PAGE

36. After listening to the cassette of *Guys and Dolls,* the show seemed to come alive just as we had seen it on opening night.

    (A) the show seemed to come alive just as we had seen it on opening night
    (B) the show was just as alive as we had seen it on opening night
    (C) just as on opening night, the show came alive
    (D) we felt the show came alive just as we had seen it on opening night
    (E) we felt it just came alive as we had seen it on opening night

37. The phenomenon of genetic fingerprinting has become crucial in the justice system, as it is more accurate than almost any of the tests previously used in crime detection.

    (A) as it is more accurate than almost any of the tests previously used in crime detection
    (B) it being more accurate than almost any of the tests previously used in crime detection
    (C) as they are more accurate than almost any of the tests previously used in crime detection
    (D) for they are more accurate than almost any of the tests previously used in crime detection
    (E) for they are being used with greater accuracy than any of the other tests used in crime detection

38. Because of fear of the spread of canine disease to the indigenous seal population, this is the reason for the proposed ban on working dogs in Antarctica.

    (A) this is the reason for the proposed ban on working dogs in Antarctica
    (B) a ban on working dogs has been proposed in Antarctica
    (C) this is why the proposed ban on working dogs is in Antarctica
    (D) a ban on dogs in Antarctica has been proposed for the working ones only
    (E) is the reason for the proposed ban on working dogs in Antarctica

GO ON TO THE NEXT PAGE

WRITING TEST—*Continued*

<u>Directions</u>: Each of the following passages is an early draft of a student essay. Some parts of the passages need to be rewritten. Read each passage and select the best answers for the questions that follow. Some questions are about particular sentences or parts of sentences and ask you to improve sentence structure and word choice. Other questions refer to parts of the essay or the entire essay and ask you to consider organization and development. In making your decisions, follow the conventions of standard written English. After you have chosen your answer, fill in the corresponding oval on your answer sheet.

<u>Questions 39-42</u> are based on the following passage.

(1) Getting a job after school was not easy. (2) First, I had to look through the papers. (3) Go to the different places to fill out applications. (4) Finally, just wait and wait to see if anyone would call me back.

(5) This was not the hardest part. (6) The hardest part came on the day that the manager called me to go to the MiniMart to take a test. (7) To see if I could add and subtract and do basic math. (8) I did my best on the test, and soon the manager called to say "You got the job." (9) I started the following week working at the cash register, and shelving food. (10) It may not have been fun. (11) I did earn some extra money for myself.

(12) My reward for all this hard work was that I could buy some things. (13) I bought a few new CDs. (14) I bought some clothes for school. (15) I also decided to put some money away for college. (16) I guess an after school job isn't so bad after all.

39. In the context of the first paragraph, which represents the best revision of sentence 3?

    (A) Going to the different places and filling out applications.
    (B) However, I had to go to the different places to fill out applications.
    (C) Next, I had to go to the different places to fill out applications.
    (D) After that, going to different places to fill out applications.
    (E) Filling out applications, different places are where I had to go next.

40. Which of the following represents the best revision of sentence 5?

    (A) However, those were not the hardest parts.
    (B) This was not to be the hardest part.
    (C) These were not the hardest part.
    (D) And, that was not the hardest part.
    (E) But, that was not the hardest part.

41. Which of the following is the best revision of the underlined portion of sentence 7 (reproduced below)?

    To see if I could add and subtract and do basic math.

    (A) The test saw if I could be adding and subtracting
    (B) They wanted to see if I could add and subtract
    (C) She wanted to see if I could add and subtract
    (D) To see me to see if I could add and subtract
    (E) To test to see if I could add and subtract

42. Which of the following represents the best way to combine sentences 10 and 11 (reproduced below)?

    It may not have been fun. I did earn some extra money for myself.

    (A) It may not have been fun, and I did earn some extra money for myself.
    (B) It may not have been fun, therefore I did earn some extra money for myself.
    (C) Although I didn't have fun, I did earn extra money for myself.
    (D) Earning extra money for myself, it made up for it not being fun.
    (E) Although not fun, earning extra money was good for me.

GO ON TO THE NEXT PAGE

WRITING TEST—*Continued*

Questions 43-46 are based on the following passage.

   (1) It's very important to be involved in an extracurricular activity. (2) This is true for a number of reasons. (3) It's good for your self-esteem. (4) It looks good on your college resume. (5) It can be a lot of fun as well.

   (6) Choosing an after school activity is a personal thing. (7) Look at your own talents. (8) Which would be best for you to be involved in? (9) Some people like to get involved in sports. (10) Some people's talents lie in the arts. (11) Are you musically inclined, or artistic? (12) And of course, there are the old standbys. (13) The school paper and the yearbook. (14) Your school may have lots of others as well. (15) Like chess club, debate team, or something else.

   (16) Look into your school's extracurricular activities. (17) You will certainly find one that interests you, and I promise that you won't regret your involvement.

43. Which of the following represents the best way to combine sentences 3, 4, and 5 (reproduced below)?

   It's good for your self-esteem. It looks good on your college resume. It can be a lot of fun as well.

   (A) It's good for your self-esteem, your college resume, and it's fun.
   (B) They can be good for your self-esteem, college resume, and be fun.
   (C) As well as being fun, they can be good for your self-esteem and college resume.
   (D) An extracurricular activity is good for your self-esteem, looks good on your college resume, and can be lots of fun.
   (E) As well as being good for your self-esteem and college resume, it can be fun as well.

44. Which of the following represents the best revision of sentence 8?

   (A) In which activity would you most like to be involved?
   (B) In what do you want to be involved?
   (C) Which would you like to be involving yourself in?
   (D) Which are best for you?
   (E) Which activity are you best to start involvement with?

45. In relation to the passage as a whole, what is the function of the last paragraph?

   (A) To give an example.
   (B) To contradict earlier information.
   (C) To evaluate the information in the second paragraph.
   (D) To introduce a new concept to the reader.
   (E) To sum up the information already presented.

46. Which of the following is the best way to combine sentences 14 and 15 (reproduced below)?

   Your school may have lots of others as well. Like chess club, debate team, or something else.

   (A) Your school may have lots of others as well as chess club, debate team, and something else.
   (B) Your school may have chess club, debate team, or something else too.
   (C) As well as those, your school may offer something else, like chess club, or debate team.
   (D) Like chess club, and debate team, your school may have lots of others as well.
   (E) Your school may also have other activities, such as chess club or debate team.

GO ON TO THE NEXT PAGE

Questions 47-50 are based on the following passage.

(1) There may be a lot of problems in our economy. (2) One place where there has been growth is with women-owned businesses. (3) People didn't typically think of women as entrepreneurs. (4) But today, the National Association of Women Business Owners—NAWBO—estimates that there are over 4.2 million businesses in the United States owned by women.

(5) The problems that confront women are not so different from men. (6) They have to face the difficulty of being entrepreneurs in a tough economy. (7) Often, they are older than the men entering the business world. (8) These can be attributes as well. (9) Women often work harder. (10) They have more realistic career goals. (11) They're more persistent. (12) They enjoy a work environment less restrictive. (13) More relaxed.

(14) If you are a woman starting out, consider entrepreneurship. (15) Assess your needs and your strengths. (16) Consider starting your own business.

47. Which of the following represents the best way to combine sentences 1 and 2 (reproduced below)?

    There may be a lot of problems in our economy. One place where there has been growth is with women-owned businesses.

    (A) There may be a lot of problems in our economy, but one area in which there has been growth is with women-owned businesses.
    (B) There may be a lot of problems in our economy, if there is one place where there is growth, it's with women in business.
    (C) The only place where there had been growth in our problem economy is with women-owned business.
    (D) There may be a lot of problems, but not in our economy with women-owned businesses.
    (E) Women-owned businesses have been the growth spot in an economy where there may have been a lot of problems.

48. Which of the following represents the best revision of sentence 5?

    (A) The problems that women face are not so different from men.
    (B) The problems that women face are not so different from those that men face.
    (C) Women's problems are not so different from men.
    (D) Problems of women are not so different from men.
    (E) Not so different from men are women's problems.

49. Which of the following sentences, if added after sentence 4, would best link it to the rest of the passage?

    (A) Women are truly the new entrepreneurs.
    (B) The growth does not come without problems, however.
    (C) That number is significant in these slow business times.
    (D) One can only be impressed by those numbers.
    (E) NAWBO estimates have not been released for this year yet.

50. Which of the following represents the best way to combine sentences 12 and 13 (reproduced below)?

    They enjoy a work environment less restricted. More relaxed.

    (A) More relaxed, they enjoy a work environment that is less restrictive.
    (B) More relaxed, they enjoy a work environment that is less restrictive than others.
    (C) They enjoy a work environment that is less restrictive and more relaxed.
    (D) A more relaxed and less restrictive environment is enjoyed by them.
    (E) Enjoying a less restrictive and more relaxed environment is what they like.

GO ON TO THE NEXT PAGE

WRITING TEST—*Continued*

Directions: The following sentences test your knowledge of grammar, usage, word choice, and idiom.

Some sentences are correct.
No sentence contains more than one error.

You will find that the error, if there is one, is underlined and lettered. Elements of the sentence that are not underlined will not be changed. In choosing answers, follow the requirements of standard written English.

If there is an error, select the one underlined part that must be changed in order to make the sentence correct, and fill in the corresponding oval on your answer sheet.

If there is no error, fill in answer oval E.

EXAMPLE:

The other delegates and him immediately
  A   B   C

accepted the resolution drafted by the
         D

neutral states. No error
      E

SAMPLE ANSWER

---

51. The reasons for Joan's move were not entirely
         A

clear—either she needed to save money and
  B
            C

she needed less space. No error
    D   E

52. The actors were exhausted, but each was able
    A   B

to remember all the complicated lines on
     C   D

opening night. No error
     E

53. Mary Anne was indebted with her mother for
        A

all the hard work her mother had done in
 B   C   D

preparation for the party. No error
       E

54. One way to determine the accuracy of
     A

reference books is to check the credentials of
     B C

its editorial board. No error
 D   E

55. After her graduation in 1989, Kate followed
    A   B

friends to New York, working at an assortment
        C

of part-time jobs before landing her first big
           D

part. No error
   E

56. The principal was aggravated by the students'
     A B   C

decision to protest during Parents' Weekend.
       D

No error
E

GO ON TO THE NEXT PAGE ➡

57. It <u>is</u> a <u>more</u> difficult task to learn to type <u>than</u>
   A B   C
<u>mastering</u> a simple word processing program.
  D
<u>No error</u>
  E

58. Many economists <u>feel that</u> taxpayers should
                 A
<u>pay less</u>, on the theory that <u>they</u> will spend
  B   C
<u>more</u> and boost the economy. <u>No error</u>
  D   E

59. None of the students <u>on the review board</u> <u>is</u>
                       A   B
qualified <u>to ascertain</u> whether or not the money
       C
was <u>well</u> spent. <u>No error</u>
  D   E

60. Educators and parents <u>agree</u> that a daily
                  A
reading time <u>will</u> not only enhance a child's
           B
education <u>but</u> also <u>helping</u> the child to read
         C   D
independently. <u>No error</u>
        E

END OF TEST

IF YOU FINISH BEFORE TIME IS CALLED, YOU MAY CHECK YOUR WORK ON EITHER PART OF THIS TEST.

HOW TO SCORE THE PRINCETON REVIEW WRITING SUBJECT TEST

When you take the real exam, the proctors will collect your text booklet and bubble sheet and send your answer sheet to New Jersey where a computer (yes, a big, old-fashioned one that has been around since the '60s) looks at the pattern of filled-in ovals on your answer sheet and gives you a score. We couldn't include even a small computer with this book, so we are providing this more primitive way of scoring your exam.

DETERMINING YOUR SCORE

STEP 1 Using the answer key on the next page, determine how many questions you got right and how many you got wrong on the test. Remember, questions that you do not answer do not count as either right answers or wrong answers.

STEP 2 List the number of right answers here.   (A) _____

STEP 3 List the number of wrong answers here. Now divide that number by 4. (Use a calculator if you're feeling particularly lazy.)   (B) _____ ÷ 4 = (C) _____

STEP 4 Subtract the number of wrong answers divided by 4 from the number of correct answers. Round this score to the nearest whole number. This is your raw score.   (A) – (C) = _____

STEP 5 To determine your real score, take the number from Step 4 above and look it up in the left column of the Score Conversion Table on page 120; the corresponding score on the right is your score on the multiple-choice section of the exam.

ANSWER KEY TO SAT II WRITING DIAGNOSTIC TEST

1. B	16. C	31. E	46. E
2. E	17. A	32. E	47. A
3. C	18. A	33. D	48. B
4. B	19. E	34. A	49. B
5. A	20. D	35. A	50. C
6. D	21. A	36. D	51. C
7. C	22. C	37. A	52. E
8. C	23. D	38. B	53. A
9. D	24. E	39. C	54. D
10. B	25. D	40. A	55. E
11. C	26. A	41. C	56. B
12. B	27. D	42. C	57. D
13. E	28. B	43. D	58. C
14. E	29. C	44. A	59. E
15. C	30. B	45. E	60. D

SAT II WRITING TEST—SCORE CONVERSION TABLE

Recentered scale as of April 1995

Raw Score	College Board Scaled Score	Raw Score	College Board Scaled Score	Raw Score	College Board Scaled Score
60	600	35	460	10	320
59	600	34	450	09	310
58	600	33	450	08	310
57	590	32	440	07	300
56	580	31	440	06	300
55	580	30	430	05	290
54	570	29	430	04	280
53	570	28	420	03	280
52	560	27	410	02	270
51	550	26	410	01	270
50	550	25	400	00	260
49	540	24	400	−01	250
48	540	23	400	−02	250
47	530	22	390	−03	240
46	530	21	380	−04	240
45	520	20	380	−05	230
44	510	19	370	−06	230
43	510	18	370	−07	220
42	500	17	360	−08	210
41	500	16	350	−09	210
40	490	15	350	−10 through −15	200
39	480	14	340		
38	480	13	340		
37	470	12	330		
36	470	11	330		

Don't forget to add in your essay score! See page 79 for explanation.

WRITING
SUBJECT TEST

SECTION 2

Your responses to the Writing Test questions should be filled in on Section Two of your answer sheet.

WRITING TEST

<table>
<tr><td>PART A</td><td>Time—20 minutes
1 Question</td><td>ESSAY</td></tr>
</table>

You have 20 minutes to write an essay on the topic assigned below. DO NOT WRITE ON ANOTHER TOPIC. AN ESSAY ON ANOTHER TOPIC IS NOT ACCEPTABLE.

The essay is assigned to give you an opportunity to show how well you can write. You should, therefore, take care to express your thoughts on the topic clearly and effectively. How well you write is much more important than how much you write, but to cover the topic adequately, you will probably need to write more than one paragraph. Be specific.

Your essay must be written on the lines provided on your answer sheet. You will receive no other paper on which to write. You will find that you have enough space if you write on every line, avoid wide margins, and keep your handwriting to a reasonable size. It is important to remember that what you write will be read by someone who is not familiar with your handwriting. Try to write or print so that what you are writing is legible to the reader.

Consider carefully the following quotation and the assignment below it. Then plan and write your essay as directed.

"In the end, the rights of the individual should precede the rights of the community."

Assignment: Do you agree or disagree? Support your position with one or more examples from history, literature, the arts, science, current events, or personal experience.

WHEN THE SUPERVISOR ANNOUNCES THAT TWENTY MINUTES HAVE PASSED, YOU MUST STOP WRITING THE ESSAY AND GO ON TO PART B IF YOU HAVE NOT ALREADY DONE SO. IF YOU FINISH YOUR ESSAY BEFORE THIS ANNOUNCEMENT, GO ON TO PART B AT ONCE.

YOU MAY MAKE NOTES ON THIS PAGE AND ON THE OPPOSITE PAGE BUT YOU MUST WRITE YOUR ESSAY ON THE ANSWER SHEET.

WRITING TEST—*Continued*

You may use this page to take notes as you plan your essay. Remember, however, that your essay MUST be written on the lined pages of the separate answer sheet.

<table>
<tr><td>PART B</td><td>Time—40 minutes
60 Questions</td><td>For each question in this part, select the best answer from among the choices given and fill in the corresponding oval on the answer sheet.</td></tr>
</table>

Directions: The following sentences test your knowledge of grammar, usage, word choice, and idiom.

    Some sentences are correct.
    No sentence contains more than one error.

You will find that the error, if there is one, is underlined and lettered. Elements of the sentence that are not underlined will not be changed. In choosing answers, follow the requirements of standard written English.

If there is an error, select the <u>one underlined part</u> that must be changed in order to make the sentence correct, and fill in the corresponding oval on your answer sheet.

If there is no error, fill in answer oval E.

EXAMPLE:

    <u>The other</u> delegates and <u>him</u> <u>immediately</u>
       A   B   C
    accepted the resolution <u>drafted by</u> the
                              D
    neutral states. <u>No error</u>
                  E

SAMPLE ANSWER

Ⓐ ⬤ Ⓒ Ⓓ Ⓔ

[E] 1. It was predicted that farmers <u>will overcome</u> the
                                 A
    decimation <u>of</u> the honeybee population
            B
    <u>by cultivating</u> other pollinators <u>such as</u> the
        C   D
    hummingbird and butterfly. <u>No error</u>
                           E

[C] 2. The ethics committee was unable <u>to come to</u> an
                                A
    agreement <u>on the legality</u> of the senator's
              B
    actions—specifically <u>him accepting</u> a gift
                      C
    <u>from a foreign diplomat</u> who was also a personal
            D
    friend. <u>No error</u>
          E

[E] tense 3. Although both the *Iliad* and *Odyssey* <u>are attributed to</u>
                                     A
    Homer, <u>there remains</u> questions <u>as to whether</u> he
              B   C
    <u>actually authored</u> the epic poems. <u>No error</u>
        D   E

[B] 4. The works of Stephen King <u>are</u> similar
                            A
    <u>to Peter Straub</u>, a fact that is not surprising <u>since</u>
         B   C
    the two men are friends and <u>have even collaborated</u>
                              D
    on a novel. <u>No error</u>
             E

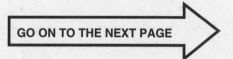

GO ON TO THE NEXT PAGE

B 5. The federal government <u>has long sought</u> a solution
                            A

toward the problem of teenage pregnancy, but
B

its efforts <u>have met with</u> limited success. <u>No error</u>
C   D   E

6. Oksana Baiul, a medal-winning figure skater in the

1994 Olympics, <u>has been admired</u> <u>for</u> how
                A   B

effortless she <u>moves</u> on the ice. <u>No error</u>
C   D   E

7. <u>Established in 1965</u>, the Housing and Urban
   A

Development Department grants <u>loan assistance for</u>
                              B

low-income housing programs and <u>encourages</u>
                                 C

<u>participation in</u> urban development projects. <u>No error</u>
D   E

8. <u>Located in southern Florida</u>, the Everglades have
   A

been damaged <u>by</u> agricultural development and
             B

urbanization, which <u>compete</u> for the water <u>on which</u>
                    C   D

the area depends. <u>No error</u>
                   E

A 9. Since World War II, the United States <u>was considered</u>
                                          A

a "superpower," a term coined <u>to describe</u> <u>those nations</u>
                              B   C

<u>possessing</u> superior economic, political, and military
D

strength. <u>No error</u>
           E

10. Today critics <u>regard</u> Jane Austen <u>as one of</u> the
                  A   B

masters of the English novel, but <u>ironically</u> <u>it</u>
                                   C   D

received little notice during her lifetime. <u>No error</u>
                                             E

11. The Industrial Revolution <u>gave birth to</u> a new
                              A

imperialism <u>in which</u> nations competed for raw
            B

materials <u>as well as</u> for new markets
          C

<u>for manufactured products</u>. <u>No error</u>
D   E

12. <u>Although</u> the number of people <u>who consider</u>
    A   B

themselves Scientologists <u>have increased</u>, the
                          C

religion continues to be viewed by many <u>with</u>
                                         D

ridicule and suspicion. <u>No error</u>
                         E

Double neg.

13. In flight, a flock of geese <u>encounters</u> <u>scarcely no</u>
                                A   B

wind resistance <u>because of</u> the "v" formation
                C

<u>it employs</u>. <u>No error</u>
D   E

14. A patient may demonstrate a marked improvement

<u>in health</u> after taking placebos, <u>despite the fact</u> that
A   B

<u>they</u> do not contain <u>any</u> medicine. <u>No error</u>
C   D   E

ambig?

GO ON TO THE NEXT PAGE

15. <u>Few</u> people <u>can contest</u> the statement that American
    A   B

sprinter and long jumper Carl Lewis is as

accomplished <u>an</u> athlete <u>than any</u>. <u>No error</u>
         C   D   E

16. <u>According to</u> Marxist theory, <u>a purely</u> socialist state
    A   B

<u>would prohibit</u> individuals <u>to own</u> private property.
    C   D

<u>No error</u>
  E

17. The <u>principle</u> doctrines of Buddhism <u>are based upon</u>
      A   B

the idea that existence is suffering <u>and that</u> the
                            C

cause of suffering <u>is</u> desire. <u>No error</u>
            D   E

18. <u>A large predatory insect</u>, the elongated body of a
          A

dragonfly can <u>often reach</u> <u>as many as</u> five inches
            B   C

<u>in length</u>. <u>No error</u>
  D   E

19. The first Progressive party, active in the presidential

election of 1912, <u>was created</u> <u>by</u> Republicans <u>which</u>
               A   B   C

supported Theodore Roosevelt <u>against</u> William Taft.
                           D

<u>No error</u>
  E

20. <u>Although</u> a tariff's purpose is <u>to increase</u> financial
    A   B

revenue by taxing imported goods, many

governments <u>have used</u> <u>them</u> to protect domestic
              C   D

industries from foreign competition. <u>No error</u>
                                    E

GO ON TO THE NEXT PAGE

Directions: In each of the following sentences, some part or all of the sentence is underlined. Below each sentence you will find five ways of phrasing the underlined part. Select the answer that produces the most effective sentence, one that is clear and exact, without awkwardness or ambiguity, and fill in the corresponding oval on your answer sheet. In choosing answers, follow the requirements of standard written English. Choose the answer that best expresses the meaning of the original sentence.

Answer (A) is always the same as the underlined part. Choose answer (A) if you think the original sentence needs no revision.

EXAMPLE:

Laura Ingalls Wilder published her first book <u>and she was sixty-five years old then</u>.

(A) and she was sixty-five years old then
(B) when she was sixty-five years old
(C) being age sixty-five years old
(D) upon the reaching of sixty-five years
(E) at the time when she was sixty-five

SAMPLE ANSWER

---

21. The most striking quality of rap music is not so much the beat that drives the melody <u>but the lyrics giving voice to inner-city slang</u>.

    (A) but the lyrics giving voice to inner-city slang
    (B) the reason being the lyrics that give voice to inner-city slang
    (C) the reason was the lyrics giving voice to inner-city slang
    (D) but the lyrics that give voice to slang from the inner city
    (E) as the lyrics that give voice to inner-city slang

22. Collective bargaining is defined as the process <u>of negotiation of a union contract or settling grievances in accord with an existing contract</u>.

    (A) of negotiation of a union contract or settling grievances in accord with an existing contract
    (B) of negotiating a union contract or, in accord with a contract in existence, settlement of grievances
    (C) of negotiating a union contract or settling grievances in accord with an existing contract
    (D) by which a union contract is negotiated or, in accord with an existing contract, grievances are being settled
    (E) by which negotiating a union contract or settling grievances in accord with an existing contract

GO ON TO THE NEXT PAGE

23. The Luna space probes were the first to enter solar orbit and photograph the far side of the moon, in 1959 they were launched.

   (A) The Luna space probes were the first to enter solar orbit and photograph the far side of the moon, in 1959 they were launched.
   (B) Launched in 1959, the Luna space probes were the first to enter solar orbit and photograph the far side of the moon.
   (C) In 1959, the first solar orbit and photograph of the far side of the moon was taking place when the Luna space probes were launched.
   (D) The launching of the Luna space probes was in 1959, the solar orbit was entered, and the far side of the moon was photographed.
   (E) The first solar orbit was when the Luna space probes were launched in 1959, and the first photograph of the far side of the moon was taken as well.

24. The reradiated energy of the sun, much of which takes the form of heat, is trapped by the layer of ozone in the atmosphere, thereby it causes higher temperatures.

   (A) atmosphere, thereby it causes higher temperatures
   (B) atmosphere it causes higher temperatures as a result
   (C) atmosphere and thereby causes higher temperatures
   (D) atmosphere; higher temperatures caused thereby
   (E) atmosphere, the higher temperatures are caused by this

25. Not only did the Sumerians make significant advances in agricultural irrigation, they also invented cuneiform writing.

   (A) they also invented cuneiform writing
   (B) they also had invented cuneiform writing
   (C) but they also invented cuneiform writing
   (D) but they also had invented cuneiform writing
   (E) as they also were inventing cuneiform writing

26. It was the publication of a Spanish letter belittling President McKinley, along with the sinking of the U.S. battleship *Maine* as well, that helped to provoke the Spanish-American War.

   (A) It was the publication of a Spanish letter belittling President McKinley, along with the sinking of the U.S. battleship *Maine* as well, that helped to provoke the Spanish-American War.
   (B) It was the publication of a Spanish letter belittling President McKinley, along with the sinking of the U.S. battleship *Maine*, helping to provoke the Spanish-American War.
   (C) The publication of a Spanish letter belittling President McKinley, along with the sinking of the U.S. battleship *Maine* as well, both were helping to provoke the Spanish-American War.
   (D) The publication of a Spanish letter belittling President McKinley, along with the sinking of the U.S. battleship *Maine*, helped to provoke the Spanish-American War.
   (E) A Spanish letter belittling President McKinley was published and the U.S. battleship *Maine* was sunk, and these helped in being the provocation to the Spanish-American War.

27. Written by Samuel Beckett, *Waiting for Godot* is a quintessential example of the theater of the absurd, combining a melancholy humor with an overwhelming sense of loss.

   (A) combining a melancholy humor with an overwhelming sense of loss
   (B) and a melancholy humor is combined with an overwhelming sense of loss
   (C) a melancholy humor and an overwhelming sense of loss are combined
   (D) for the combination of a melancholy humor and an overwhelming sense of loss
   (E) and with this was the combination of a melancholy humor with an overwhelming sense of loss

GO ON TO THE NEXT PAGE →

28. Hailed as one of the greatest female poets of all time, <u>Emily Dickinson's poems range in subject matter from love and nature to death and immortality</u>.

    (A) Emily Dickinson's poems range in subject matter from love and nature to death and immortality
    (B) Emily Dickinson's poems ranged in subject matter from love and nature to death and immortality
    (C) Emily Dickinson's poems have a subject matter that ranges from love and nature to death and immortality
    (D) Emily Dickinson wrote poems ranging in subject matter from love and nature to death and immortality
    (E) Emily Dickinson had written poems that were ranging in subject matter from love and nature to death and immortality

29. Angel Cordero, one of the most successful jockeys in history, won over seven thousand races during his twenty-two-year <u>career, this includes three Kentucky Derby victories</u>.

    (A) career, this includes three Kentucky Derby victories
    (B) career, being included three Kentucky Derby victories
    (C) career, whose victories include three Kentucky Derbies
    (D) career; his victories include three Kentucky Derbies
    (E) career, these victories of his include three Kentucky Derbies

30. Typically, the social organization of an ant colony is based upon different castes, <u>each with a specific duty to fulfill</u>.

    (A) each with a specific duty to fulfill
    (B) each having their specific duty to fulfill
    (C) when they each have their own duty to fulfill
    (D) which has a specific duty to fulfill
    (E) they each have a specific duty to fulfill

31. A sacred plant in China and Japan, the ginkgo tree is highly valued in the United States and Europe because <u>of its tolerance for smoke, low temperatures, and it needs little water</u>.

    (A) of its tolerance for smoke, low temperatures, and it needs little water
    (B) of its tolerance for smoke and low temperatures and its need for water is very little
    (C) it can tolerate smoke, low temperatures, and needs little water
    (D) it can tolerate smoke, withstanding low temperatures, and needs little water
    (E) it can tolerate smoke, withstand low temperatures, and survive with little water

32. Both literary critics and the general public describe *Catcher in the Rye* as one of American literature's greatest novels, <u>but J. D. Salinger seems indifferent about his success</u>.

    (A) but J. D. Salinger seems indifferent about his success
    (B) while J. D. Salinger seems indifferent about his success
    (C) and J. D. Salinger seems indifferent to his success
    (D) so that J. D. Salinger seems indifferent to his success
    (E) but J. D. Salinger seems indifferent to his success

GO ON TO THE NEXT PAGE

33. Each year thousands of newlyweds visit the internationally famous Niagara Falls, which were formed over ten thousand years ago.

    (A) Each year thousands of newlyweds visit the internationally famous Niagara Falls, which were formed over ten thousand years ago.
    (B) Formed over ten thousand years ago, thousands of newlyweds visit the internationally famous Niagara Falls each year.
    (C) Thousands of newlyweds visit the internationally famous Niagara Falls each year, being formed over ten thousand years ago.
    (D) Thousands of newlyweds had visited the internationally famous Niagara Falls each year, which were formed over ten thousand years ago.
    (E) Each year, forming over ten thousand years ago, the Niagara Falls are visited by thousands of newlyweds.

34. The diet of a koala bear consisting of only one species of eucalyptus at a particular stage of maturation.

    (A) The diet of a koala bear consisting of
    (B) The koala bear with its diet having consisted of
    (C) Consisting of the diet of a koala bear is
    (D) It is the diet of a koala bear consisting of
    (E) The diet of a koala bear consists of

35. In economic terms, a secret agreement among two people to defraud a third person or injuring him is known as collusion.

    (A) among two people to defraud a third person or injuring him
    (B) among two people to defraud a third person or causing injury to him
    (C) among two people defrauding a third person or their injuring him
    (D) between two people to defraud a third person or injure him
    (E) between two people in the defrauding of a third person or the injury of him

36. Using garish and artificial colors, the works of Henri de Toulouse-Lautrec depicted the life of music halls, cabarets, and circuses with a new immediacy.

    (A) the works of Henri de Toulouse-Lautrec depicted the life of music halls, cabarets, and circuses with a new immediacy
    (B) Henri de Toulouse-Lautrec's works have depicted with a new immediacy the life of music halls, cabarets, and circuses
    (C) Henri de Toulouse-Lautrec depicted the life of music halls, cabarets, and circuses with a new immediacy
    (D) Henri de Toulouse-Lautrec depicting the life of music halls, cabarets, and circuses with a new immediacy
    (E) depicting with a new immediacy the life of music halls, cabarets, and circuses was Henri de Toulouse-Lautrec

GO ON TO THE NEXT PAGE

37. In T. H. White's novel *The Once and Future King*, the character of Arthur he seeks to establish the rule of law as well as unite the rival factions under it.

    (A) the character of Arthur he seeks to establish the rule of law as well as unite the rival factions under it

    (B) the character of Arthur seeks to establish the rule of law as well as uniting the rival factions under it

    (C) the character Arthur seeks to establish the rule of law as well as unite the rival factions under him

    (D) the character Arthur he seeks the establishment of the rule of law as well as uniting the rival factions under him

    (E) the character Arthur seeks the establishment of the rule of law and the unification of the rival factions under it

38. Both the FBI and the CIA are responsible to counterintelligence operations, and the CIA focuses primarily on those activities outside the United States.

    (A) to counterintelligence operations, and the CIA focuses primarily

    (B) for counterintelligence operations, but the CIA focuses primarily

    (C) for counterintelligence operations, but primarily the CIA's focus

    (D) to counterintelligence operations, but the primary focus of the CIA is

    (E) for counterintelligence operations, but the primary focus of the CIA is

GO ON TO THE NEXT PAGE

WRITING TEST—*Continued*

Directions: Each of the following passages is an early draft of a student essay. Some parts of the passages need to be rewritten. Read each passage and select the best answer for the questions that follow. Some questions are about particular sentences or parts of sentences and ask you to improve sentence structure and word choice. Other questions refer to parts of the essay or the entire essay and ask you to consider organization and development. In making your decisions, follow the conventions of standard written English. After you have chosen your answer, fill in the corresponding oval on your answer sheet.

Questions 39-44 are based on the following passage.

(1) I used to have an irrational fear of bees. (2) Anytime I heard a buzzing sound, my heart would start to beat faster and faster. (3) Sometimes breathing was hard.

(4) I've always loved working in my garden. (5) But once spring came around, all the bees came out. (6) I was terrified of going outside. (7) My garden began to wither away. (8) Finally, I decided to do something about it. (9) I called up my friend Anne. (10) Her uncle happens to be a bee keeper. (11) I wanted to ask if I could meet him. (12) Anne's uncle agreed to take me to his hives the next day. (13) From the second I woke up that day, I was petrified, but luckily, Anne's uncle was very understanding. (14) He suited me up in beekeeping gear so that I couldn't get stung, and then he showed me his bee hives.

(15) To my surprise, I found myself fascinated by them. (16) Anne's uncle described how the bees are organized in castes, how they act as pollinators, and how they make honey. (17) I was so interested by what he said that I went to the library that very night and researched bees for hours. (18) And now—now I can't keep away from bees. (19) Each morning, I have visited Anne's uncle helping out with the hives, while in the afternoon, I devote my time to my garden surrounded by bees.

39. Which of the following is the best way to revise the underlined portions of sentences 2 and 3 (reproduced below) so that the two sentences are combined into one?

    Anytime I heard a buzzing sound, my heart would start to beat faster and faster. Sometimes breathing was hard.

    (A) faster, but sometimes breathing was hard
    (B) faster, and sometimes I would find it hard to breathe
    (C) faster, and sometimes harder to breathe
    (D) faster, so sometimes finding it hard to breathe
    (E) faster, while sometimes it was breathing that was hard

40. Which of the following sentences, if added after sentence 3, would best link the first paragraph with the rest of the essay?

    (A) It seems that I have had this fear of bees for an eternity.
    (B) There were even times that I couldn't move my body, so intense was my fear of bees.
    (C) Unfortunately, my fear of bees wasn't a problem I could ignore because of my garden.
    (D) Usually, gardening is a pleasurable experience.
    (E) I try not to be afraid of bees, but in my garden, it's impossible.

41. Which of the following is the best way to revise and combine sentences 6 and 7 (reproduced below)?

    I was terrified of going outside. My garden began to wither away.

    (A) Being terrified of going outside, my garden began to wither away
    (B) Though going outside terrified me, my garden began to wither away.
    (C) Since going outside did terrify me, it was then my garden began to wither away.
    (D) Going outside terrified me, and as a result, my garden began to wither away.
    (E) My garden, withering away, as I was terrified of going outside.

42. The phrase "to do something about it" in sentence 8 can best be made more specific if rewritten as

    (A) to make my garden grow again
    (B) to learn more about bees
    (C) to get in touch with a beekeeper
    (D) to combat my fear of bees
    (E) to reconsider my feelings

GO ON TO THE NEXT PAGE

43. To vary the pattern of short sentences in the second paragraph, which of the following would be the best way to combine sentences 10 and 11 (reproduced below)?

Her uncle happens to be a beekeeper. I wanted to ask if I could meet him.

(A) Her uncle happens to be a beekeeper, which made me ask if I could meet with him.
(B) As her uncle is a beekeeper, a meeting with him I wanted to ask.
(C) Her uncle being a beekeeper, I wanted to ask if my meeting him was possible.
(D) I wanted to ask if I could meet, seeing that he happens to be a beekeeper, her uncle.
(E) I wanted to ask if I could meet her uncle, who happens to be a beekeeper.

44. In the context of the third paragraph, which of the following is the best version of the underlined portion of sentence 19 (reproduced below)?

Each morning, I have visited Anne's uncle helping out with the hives, while in the afternoon, I devote my time to my garden surrounded by bees.

(A) (as it is now)
(B) I visit Anne's uncle to help out
(C) having visited Anne's uncle and helping out
(D) visiting Anne's uncle to help out
(E) visiting Anne's uncle has helped out

GO ON TO THE NEXT PAGE

Questions 45-50. The following passage was written in response to an assignment to write an editorial on voting.

(1) Are today's voters more apathetic than those in previous years? (2) Sadly, the answer seems to be "yes." (3) Living in this country where we have freedoms we take for granted, the right to vote is no longer viewed as the privilege it is meant to be.

(4) In the early nineteenth century, voter apathy did not seem to exist. (5) In fact, in presidential elections, voter participation was usually higher than 95 percent. (6) It was just as high, if not higher, for elections at the local level. (7) Now compare these statistics: today, voter participation is less than 50 percent. (8) It is even lower for local elections. (9) Why voter apathy is so great no one can determine for sure. (10) Political scientists have put forth some ideas. (11) Regardless, we need to revitalize the public, to make people feel that voting is an integral part of living in this nation. (12) And we need to educate, to let people know that voting does mean something and that it can make a change.

(13) Our government is supposed to be by, for, and of the people. (14) It may take time and more than a little effort, but if we will have striven for this goal now, our future can only be brighter.

45. Which of the following is the best way to revise the underlined portion of sentence 3 (reproduced below)?

    Living in this country where we have freedoms we take for granted, the right to vote is no longer viewed as the privilege it is meant to be.

    (A) Living in this country where we have freedoms we take for granted, it is the right to vote that is no longer viewed
    (B) No longer viewing the right to vote, we live in this country where freedoms are taken for granted
    (C) Taking freedoms for granted and living in this country, the right to vote is no longer viewed
    (D) We live in this country where freedoms are taken for granted, it is the right to vote that is no longer viewed
    (E) Living in this country where freedoms are taken for granted, we no longer view the right to vote

46. The writer of the passage could best improve sentence 10 by

    (A) including possible reasons
    (B) suggesting ways to increase voter participation
    (C) discussing the implications of voter apathy
    (D) explaining the idea of the vote as a privilege
    (E) providing personal opinions

47. Which of the following would be the best replacement for "*And*" at the beginning of sentence 12 (reproduced below)?

    And we need to educate, to let people know that voting does mean something and that it can make a change.

    (A) Except for this,
    (B) Nonetheless,
    (C) Moreover,
    (D) Rather,
    (E) For example,

48. Which of the following sentences, if added before sentence 13, would best link the third paragraph with the rest of the essay?

    (A) In this country, we have a democratic government.
    (B) We must take the initiative to increase voter participation because this country was founded on a democratic ideal.
    (C) Voting is an incredibly important part of any democracy; this is a fact we cannot dismiss.
    (D) It is unacceptable that we have such a low level of voter participation.
    (E) Voter apathy will only increase if we are not careful.

GO ON TO THE NEXT PAGE

49. Which of the following versions of the underlined portion of sentence 14 (reproduced below) is best?

    It may take time and more than a little effort, <u>but if we will have striven</u> for this goal now, our future can only be brighter.

    (A) (as it is now)
    (B) and if we will be striving
    (C) but if we also strive
    (D) but if we strive
    (E) however, if we do strive

50. All of the following strategies are used by the writer of the passage EXCEPT

    (A) employing a historical reference
    (B) picking specific examples
    (C) suggesting solutions to a problem
    (D) answering a question
    (E) introducing an assumption

GO ON TO THE NEXT PAGE

Directions: The following sentences test your knowledge of grammar, usage, word choice, and idiom.

Some sentences are correct.
No sentence contains more than one error.

You will find that the error, if there is one, is underlined and lettered. Elements of the sentence that are not underlined will not be changed. In choosing answers, follow the requirements of standard written English.

If there is an error, select the <u>one underlined part</u> that must be changed in order to make the sentence correct, and fill in the corresponding oval on your answer sheet.

If there is no error, fill in answer oval E.

EXAMPLE:

<u>The other</u> delegates and <u>him</u> <u>immediately</u>
    A   B   C

accepted the resolution <u>drafted by</u> the
                              D

neutral states. <u>No error</u>
                E

SAMPLE ANSWER
Ⓐ●ⒸⒹⒺ

---

51. Since 1969, <u>less than</u> three women <u>have won</u> the
              A   B

    four tournaments <u>that make up</u> tennis's
                    C

    <u>highly touted</u> "Grand Slam." <u>No error</u>
        D   E

52. By definition, chemotherapy <u>is</u> the treatment of a
                         A

    disease <u>with</u> chemicals or drugs, but in everyday
           B

    usage, it <u>most often</u> <u>refers to</u> the treatment of
              C   D

    cancer. <u>No error</u>
          E

53. Inside the larynx, commonly <u>known as</u> the voice
                         A

    box, <u>is</u> the vocal cords, a pair of elastic folds
         B

    <u>which vibrate</u> <u>to produce sound</u>. <u>No error</u>
        C   D   E

54. Malaria <u>is transmitted by</u> the *Anopheles* mosquito,
              A

    which <u>transfers</u> the *Plasmodium* parasite <u>from</u> the
           B   C

    blood of an infected person to <u>a healthy person</u>.
                               D

    <u>No error</u>
       E

55. <u>Though</u> thousands of college basketball players
    A

    may dream <u>of becoming</u> <u>a member</u> of the NBA, few
             B   C

    <u>will ever reach</u> that goal. <u>No error</u>
        D   E

56. <u>A depression</u> <u>is defined as</u> a period of crisis
    A   B

    <u>characterized by</u> falling prices, <u>reduced production</u>,
        C   D

    and high unemployment. <u>No error</u>
                         E

GO ON TO THE NEXT PAGE

57. <u>Attaining</u> <u>speeds</u> of over sixty miles per hour,
    A   B

    cheetahs are the <u>much faster</u> <u>of</u> all four-footed
          C   D

    animals. <u>No error</u>
        E

58. Researchers <u>are increasing</u> <u>their</u> efforts to fight the
         A   B

    Ebola virus, <u>now that</u> the disease <u>spread to</u> the
         C   D

    human population in Africa. <u>No error</u>
           E

59. An individual <u>who suffers from</u> obsessive-
          A

    compulsive personality disorder often recognizes

    <u>their</u> behavior as problematic, but <u>is</u> still unable
    B   C

    <u>to control</u> it. <u>No error</u>
    D   E

60. Some ballet dancers <u>are noted</u> more for <u>their</u>
          A   B

    strength <u>and not</u> for their agility <u>or</u> flexibility.
        C   D

    <u>No error</u>
    E

END OF TEST

IF YOU FINISH BEFORE TIME IS CALLED, YOU MAY CHECK YOUR WORK ON EITHER PART OF THIS TEST.

HOW TO SCORE THE PRINCETON REVIEW WRITING SUBJECT TEST

When you take the real exam, the proctors will collect your text booklet and bubble sheet and send your answer sheet to New Jersey where a computer (yes, a big, old-fashioned one that has been around since the '60s) looks at the pattern of filled-in ovals on your answer sheet and gives you a score. We couldn't include even a small computer with this book, so we are providing this more primitive way of scoring your exam.

DETERMINING YOUR SCORE

STEP 1   Using the answer key on the next page, determine how many questions you got right and how many you got wrong on the test. Remember, questions that you do not answer do not count as either right answers or wrong answers.

STEP 2   List the number of right answers here.

(A) _____

STEP 3   List the number of wrong answers here. Now divide that number by 4. (Use a calculator if you're feeling particularly lazy.)

(B) _____ ÷ 4 = (C) _____

STEP 4   Subtract the number of wrong answers divided by 4 from the number of correct answers. Round this score to the nearest whole number. This is your raw score.

(A) – (C) = _____

STEP 5   To determine your real score, take the number from Step 4 above and look it up in the left column of the Score Conversion Table on page 142; the corresponding score on the right is your score on the multiple-choice section of the exam.

ANSWER KEY TO SAT II WRITING DIAGNOSTIC TEST

1. A	16. D	31. E	46. A
2. C	17. A	32. E	47. C
3. B	18. A	33. A	48. B
4. B	19. C	34. E	49. D
5. B	20. D	35. D	50. E
6. C	21. E	36. C	51. A
7. E	22. C	37. C	52. E
8. E	23. B	38. B	53. B
9. A	24. C	39. B	54. D
10. D	25. C	40. C	55. C
11. E	26. D	41. D	56. E
12. C	27. A	42. D	57. C
13. B	28. D	43. E	58. D
14. E	29. D	44. B	59. B
15. D	30. A	45. E	60. C

SAT II WRITING TEST—SCORE CONVERSION TABLE

Recentered scale as of April 1995

Raw Score	College Board Scaled Score	Raw Score	College Board Scaled Score	Raw Score	College Board Scaled Score
60	600	35	460	10	320
59	600	34	450	09	310
58	600	33	450	08	310
57	590	32	440	07	300
56	580	31	440	06	300
55	580	30	430	05	290
54	570	29	430	04	280
53	570	28	420	03	280
52	560	27	410	02	270
51	550	26	410	01	270
50	550	25	400	00	260
49	540	24	400	−01	250
48	540	23	400	−02	250
47	530	22	390	−03	240
46	530	21	380	−04	240
45	520	20	380	−05	230
44	510	19	370	−06	230
43	510	18	370	−07	220
42	500	17	360	−08	210
41	500	16	350	−09	210
40	490	15	350	−10 through −15	200
39	480	14	340		
38	480	13	340		
37	470	12	330		
36	470	11	330		

Don't forget to add in your essay score! See page 79 for explanation.

WRITING
SUBJECT TEST

SECTION 3

Your responses to the Writing Test questions should be filled in on Section Three of your answer sheet.

WRITING TEST

You have 20 minutes to write an essay on the topic assigned below. DO NOT WRITE ON ANOTHER TOPIC. AN ESSAY ON ANOTHER TOPIC IS NOT ACCEPTABLE.

The essay is assigned to give you an opportunity to show how well you can write. You should, therefore, take care to express your thoughts on the topic clearly and effectively. How well you write is much more important than how much you write, but to cover the topic adequately, you will probably need to write more than one paragraph. Be specific.

Your essay must be written on the lines provided on your answer sheet. You will receive no other paper on which to write. You will find that you have enough space if you write on every line, avoid wide margins, and keep your handwriting to a reasonable size. It is important to remember that what you write will be read by someone who is not familiar with your handwriting. Try to write or print so that what you are writing is legible to the reader.

Consider carefully the following quotation and the assignment below it. Then plan and write your essay as directed.

"The love of money is the root of all evil."

Assignment: Choose a specific example from personal experience, current events, or from your reading in history, literature, or other subjects and use this example as the basis for an essay in which you agree or disagree with the statement above. Be sure to be specific.

WHEN THE SUPERVISOR ANNOUNCES THAT TWENTY MINUTES HAVE PASSED, YOU MUST STOP WRITING THE ESSAY AND GO ON TO PART B IF YOU HAVE NOT ALREADY DONE SO. IF YOU FINISH YOUR ESSAY BEFORE THIS ANNOUNCEMENT, GO ON TO PART B AT ONCE.

YOU MAY MAKE NOTES ON THIS PAGE AND ON THE OPPOSITE PAGE BUT YOU MUST WRITE YOUR ESSAY ON THE ANSWER SHEET.

WRITING TEST—*Continued*

You may use this page to take notes as you plan your essay. Remember, however, that your essay MUST be written on the lined pages of the separate answer sheet.

WRITING TEST—*Continued*

PART B   Time—40 minutes   For each question in this part, select the best answer from among
60 Questions   the choices given and fill in the corresponding oval on the answer
sheet.

Directions: The following sentences test your knowledge of grammar, usage, word choice, and idiom.

Some sentences are correct.
No sentence contains more than one error.

You will find that the error, if there is one, is underlined and lettered. Elements of the sentence that are not underlined will not be changed. In choosing answers, follow the requirements of standard written English.

If there is an error, select the one underlined part that must be changed in order to make the sentence correct, and fill in the corresponding oval on your answer sheet.

If there is no error, fill in answer oval E.

EXAMPLE:

The other delegates and him immediately
    A   B   C

accepted the resolution drafted by the
                  D

neutral states. No error
          E

SAMPLE ANSWER
Ⓐ ● Ⓒ Ⓓ Ⓔ

1. The Basque people inhabit the Pyrenees mountains,
                  A

which lie between France and Spain, and speak
   B

their own language, called Euskera. No error
   C   D   E

2. The effects of the medication were so severe that
                        A   B

Jane couldn't hardly raise her right arm. No error
     C   D   E

3. The government's proposal to raise the minimum
                   A

wage was met with great opposition by those who
      B   C

felt that they may hurt small businesses. No error
   D   E

4. Amy was certain that the key to happiness was
       A

to be found more in helping others and not in
    B   C

helping herself. No error
      D   E

5. According to legend, visitors who toss coins over
                   A

their shoulders into the basin of the Fontana di
   B

Trevi, Rome's largest fountain, will return to Rome
            C   D

someday. No error
      E

GO ON TO THE NEXT PAGE

A 6. Throughout history, <u>there is</u> many true heroes:
          A

  people <u>who have</u> inspired us <u>with their</u> courage,
        B   C

  honor, <u>and strength</u>. <u>No error</u>
         D   E

A 7. Few of the people <u>which</u> were attending the rally
               A

  <u>on the campus</u> green <u>were able</u> to hear the speakers
      B   C

  <u>clearly</u>. <u>No error</u>
    D   E

A 8. Theta 1 C, the <u>brighter of</u> the four Trapezium stars,
            A

  <u>provides</u> 99 percent of the light in the Orion nebula—
    B

  one <u>of the few nebulas</u> that <u>can be seen</u> by the
       C   D

  naked eye. <u>No error</u>
         E

E 9. <u>Not only</u> is <u>solving crossword</u> puzzles an
     A   B

  intellectual challenge, but <u>it is</u> also a great way
                    C

  <u>to pass</u> the time. <u>No error</u>
    D   E

D 10. <u>A great Indian leader</u>, Mohandas Ghandi <u>believed</u>
       A   B

  that nonviolent resistance, or *satyagraha*, <u>was</u> as
                           C

  effective <u>than violence</u>. <u>No error</u>
        D   E

A 11. A panel made up of shopkeepers, parents, and

  concerned homeowners <u>have come</u> together
                A

  <u>to protest</u> the school <u>tax increase</u> <u>proposed</u> for this
    B   C   D

  year. <u>No error</u>
     E

D 12. Modern hospitals <u>use both</u> expensive diagnostic
              A

  machines and the expertise <u>of doctors</u>, nurses, and
                    B

  staff <u>to insure</u> that <u>it will give</u> the most effective
      C   D

  treatment to patients. <u>No error</u>
            E

A 13. Even though she read <u>very quick</u>, Marie
              A

  <u>was not able</u> to <u>comprehend the assignment</u> and
      B   C

  <u>complete</u> her homework. <u>No error</u>
    D   E

D 14. Ms. Franco <u>informed</u> the introductory Italian class
         A

  that <u>its incoming</u> language skills <u>were superior</u> to
       B   C

  <u>last year's class</u>. <u>No error</u>
    D   E

15. <u>Because</u> he has a <u>commitment with</u> local economic
   A   B

  issues, <u>our town councilman</u> has sent <u>each of his</u>
        C   D

  constituents a pamphlet with information on saving

  money. <u>No error</u>
        E

C 16. Even though <u>she trained</u> for several weeks before
           A

  <u>her meet</u>, Marie was sure that she <u>could of run</u> a
    B   C

  much better race <u>than she did</u> on Saturday.
             D

  <u>No error</u>
   E

GO ON TO THE NEXT PAGE →

17. The number of men <u>who are</u> considered
                        A
    <u>the primary caretaker</u> of <u>their children</u> has
                B   C
    <u>increased significantly</u> in the last twenty years.
                    D
    <u>No error</u>
        E

18. People <u>have played</u> musical instruments since
                A
    prehistoric times, <u>picking up shells</u>, bones, and
                            B
    sticks and <u>using it</u> to produce <u>basic rhythms</u>.
                    C   D
    <u>No error</u>
        E

19. Isadora Duncan, one <u>of the pioneers</u> of American
                            A
    modern dance, <u>was famous</u> for her style,
                        B
    <u>which borrowed</u> extensively from
            C
    <u>that of the ancient Greeks</u>. <u>No error</u>
                D   E

20. <u>After Rosa Parks</u> was arrested <u>from not giving</u> up
            A   B
    her seat on a bus to a white person, African

    Americans in Montgomery, Alabama <u>began</u> a bus
                                        C
    boycott <u>that lasted</u> for a full year. <u>No error</u>
                D   E

GO ON TO THE NEXT PAGE

<u>Directions</u>: In each of the following sentences some part or all of the sentence is underlined. Below each sentence you will find five ways of phrasing the underlined part. Select the answer that produces the most effective sentence, one that is clear and exact, without awkwardness or ambiguity, and fill in the corresponding oval on your answer sheet. In choosing answers, follow the requirements of standard written English. Choose the answer that best expresses the meaning of the original sentence.

Answer (A) is always the same as the underlined part. Choose answer (A) if you think the original sentence needs no revision.

EXAMPLE:

Laura Ingalls Wilder published her first book <u>and she was sixty-five years old then</u>.

(A) and she was sixty-five years old then
(B) when she was sixty-five years old
(C) being age sixty-five years old
(D) upon the reaching of sixty-five years
(E) at the time when she was sixty-five

SAMPLE ANSWER

---

21. Franklin was nervous about the speech he had to give, <u>this</u> nervousness helped to make him perform even better than he had expected.

    (A) this
    (B) furthermore
    (C) but this
    (D) for which
    (E) that

22. <u>One of the earliest complete code of laws compiling King Hammurabi</u>, a Babylonian ruler, over three thousand years ago.

    (A) One of the earliest complete code of laws compiling King Hammurabi
    (B) Among the earliest of complete codes of laws compiled by King Hammurabi
    (C) One of the earliest complete code of laws was compiled by King Hammurabi
    (D) King Hammurabi, compiler of one of the earliest complete code of laws
    (E) King Hammurabi compiled one of the earliest complete code of laws

23. <u>In the 1820s, an empire in Natal formed by the Zulus had lasted until 1879.</u>

    (A) In the 1820s, an empire in Natal formed by the Zulus had lasted until 1879.
    (B) In the 1820s, the Zulu empire, which lasted until 1879, was formed in Natal.
    (C) In Natal in the 1820s, formed the Zulus, was the empire lasting until 1879.
    (D) Forming in the 1820s in Natal, it was the Zulu empire that had lasted until 1879.
    (E) The Zulus in the 1820s had formed an empire, and the empire it lasted until 1879.

GO ON TO THE NEXT PAGE

24. During her first year of study, <u>the observation of David Greybeard, a chimp, eating a baby bush-pig gave Jane Goodall the proof she needed that chimps are carnivorous</u>.

    (A) the observation of David Greybeard, a chimp, eating a baby bush-pig gave Jane Goodall the proof she needed that chimps are carnivorous
    (B) the observation of a chimp named David Greybeard eating a baby bush-pig gave to Jane Goodall the proof that chimps are carnivorous
    (C) the observation of the eating of a baby bush-pig by David Greybeard, a chimp, proved to Jane Goodall that chimps are carnivorous.
    (D) Jane Goodall observed David Greybeard, a chimp, eat a baby bush-pig, proving that chimps are carnivorous
    (E) Jane Goodall was observing a chimp named David Greybeard eat a baby bush-pig, proof that chimps are carnivorous

25. The number of tabloids in the supermarket sometimes makes it difficult for a consumer to distinguish <u>true facts from those that are made up</u>.

    (A) true facts from those that are made up
    (B) truth from fiction
    (C) true facts from made up facts
    (D) facts that are made up from those that are true
    (E) facts from each other

26. When James Naismith invented basketball in 1891, <u>ideas from games like hockey, soccer, and even football were used, but also ideas were added by him</u>.

    (A) ideas from games like hockey, soccer, and even football were used, but also ideas were added by him
    (B) ideas from games like hockey, soccer, and even football were used, but it was added to by his own ideas.
    (C) ideas from games such as hockey, soccer, and even football were used by him with his own ideas.
    (D) he used ideas from games such as hockey, soccer, and even football along with his own ideas.
    (E) he used his own ideas and games like hockey, soccer, and even football.

27. Though all of the contestants had submitted wonderful essays on the same topic, <u>each essay had its own personality</u>.

    (A) each essay had its own personality
    (B) each essay had their own personalities
    (C) with each there was their own personality
    (D) which had its own personality
    (E) they each had personalities of their own

28. When Joan of Arc was only seventeen, she heard voices that inspired her to lead the army <u>as well as freeing France from the English</u>.

    (A) as well as freeing France from the English
    (B) and she also freed France from England
    (C) as well as to free France from the English
    (D) the freeing of France from the English also being accomplished by her
    (E) together with the freeing of France from the English

29. Frank likes to play field hockey not so much for the competition <u>but for its being a valuable form of exercise</u>.

    (A) but for its being a valuable form of exercise
    (B) but the reason is that it is valuable exercise
    (C) the reason being its value as exercise
    (D) but because its exercise is valuable
    (E) as for the exercise

30. Mr. Waldner's troop was required to do a certain amount of community <u>service: this being that they had to</u> volunteer time at one of our shelters or to a local charity.

    (A) service: this being that they had to
    (B) service, this as
    (C) service, these things had to be
    (D) service; it had to
    (E) service; that being

GO ON TO THE NEXT PAGE

31. Feeding your pet too much food is as unhealthy <u>than if you feed</u> it too little.

    (A) than if you feed
    (B) as feeding
    (C) as if one feed
    (D) than it could be by feeding
    (E) as for feeding

32. The approval of the committee was held up by <u>red tape, therefore they held up the start of our new project</u>.

    (A) red tape, therefore they held up the start of our new project
    (B) red tape they held up the start of our new project
    (C) red tape, which held up the start of our new project
    (D) red tape; the start of our new project getting held up
    (E) red tape, the start of our project being held up by that

33. The performance on Saturday night was better than any of the performers could have <u>imagined, having received</u> a standing ovation from the enthusiastic crowd.

    (A) imagined, having received
    (B) imagined; they had to receive
    (C) imagined; they received
    (D) imagined: including the reception of
    (E) imagined and so they received

34. Women attending the annual Writer's Conference this year will have an opportunity to attend special seminars <u>and hearing readings</u> by women authors.

    (A) and hearing readings
    (B) and to hear readings
    (C) as well as hearing readings
    (D) and also hearing readings
    (E) in addition the women will be hearing readings

35. Although the number of companies <u>that offer retraining for workers has increased, there is still much</u> to be done to help the displaced learn new skills.

    (A) that offer retraining for workers has increased, there is still much
    (B) offering worker retraining has increased, there are many things still needing
    (C) that offer retraining for workers have increased, much remains
    (D) offering retraining for workers have increased, there is still much
    (E) that offer workers retraining have increased, many things remain

36. <u>After a particularly warm winter, with practically no snow, the hotels in town were hoping to regain some of their lost revenue by offering bargain packages.</u>

    (A) After a particularly warm winter, with practically no snow, the hotels in town were hoping to regain some of their lost revenue by offering bargain packages.
    (B) Hoping to regain some of their lost revenue, the lack of snow due to the warm winter led the hotels in town to offer bargain packages.
    (C) The offering of bargain packages by the hotels in town, hoping to regain some of their lost revenue after a particularly warm, snowless winter.
    (D) The hotels in town are offering bargain packages by hoping to regain some of the lost revenue due to warm weather with very little snow.
    (E) By offering a bargain package due to the warm weather and lack of snow, the hope is to regain some lost revenue for the hotels in town.

GO ON TO THE NEXT PAGE →

37. A city renowned for its magnificent architecture, <u>visitors to Florence enjoy staying in villas, former palaces, and monasteries</u>.

    (A) visitors to Florence enjoy staying in villas, former palaces, and monasteries
    (B) visitors of Florence like to stay in villas, former palaces, and monasteries
    (C) those who visit Florence like to stay in villas, former palaces, and monasteries
    (D) Florence offers villas, former palaces, and monasteries as accommodations for its visitors
    (E) Florence, the home of villas, former palaces, and monasteries, has its visitors stay there

38. Before the advent of the printing press, books were written out by <u>hand so it was very expensive</u>.

    (A) hand so it was very expensive
    (B) hand, therefore it was very expensive
    (C) hand; that is why it was very expensive
    (D) hand, the reason being that they were very expensive
    (E) hand; as a result they were very expensive

GO ON TO THE NEXT PAGE

WRITING TEST—*Continued*

Directions: Each of the following passages is an early draft of a student essay. Some part of the passages need to be rewritten. Read each passage and select the best answers for the question that follow. Some questions are about particular sentences or parts of sentences and ask you to improve sentence structure and word choice. Other questions refer to parts of the essay or the entire essay and ask you to consider organization and development. In making your decisions, follow the conventions of standard written English, fill in the corresponding oval in your answer sheet.

Questions 39-44 are based on the following passage.

(1) I never thought I'd be interested in volunteer work. (2) My friends volunteered. (3) I never did. (4) Our school instituted a program to get students to volunteer. (5) They sent a list of ideas to the students.

(6) I have lots of brothers and sisters. (7) I'm used to being around children. (8) When I saw the Big Brothers Big Sisters charity listed, it caught my interest. (9) Their motto is "Every kid needs a hero." (10) It wasn't easy to become a big sister. (11) You have to be eighteen. (12) You have to be interviewed and trained. (13) But, soon, my caseworker calls to tell me that I had been assigned a little sister.

(14) The night before I was to meet Janie, my "little," I could hardly sleep. (15) I took the bus to her apartment. (16) We went to the park and spent a quiet day feeding the ducks and talking. (17) That night, I went to sleep knowing that I had begun to make a difference in one person's life.

39. Which of the following would be the best way to combine sentences 2 and 3 (reproduced below) into one?

    My friends volunteered. I never did.

    (A) volunteered and I never did
    (B) volunteered, but I never did
    (C) volunteered, but unlike them, I never did
    (D) volunteered, so I, unlike them, never did
    (E) volunteered, while I didn't ever

40. Which of the following sentences, if added to the end of the first paragraph would best connect it to the rest of the essay?

    (A) However, I remained skeptical.
    (B) It contained names of all the local charity organizations.
    (C) Unfortunately, many of the charities listed didn't interest me.
    (D) One got my attention.
    (E) Therefore, I gave some thought to volunteer work.

41. Which of the following would be the best way to combine sentences 11 and 12 (reproduced below) so as to vary the pattern of several short sentences in a row?

    You have to be eighteen. You have to be interviewed and trained.

    (A) Not only being eighteen, but interviewed, and trained.
    (B) You have to be eighteen, interviewed, and trained.
    (C) Interviewed and trained, you must be eighteen as well.
    (D) In addition to being eighteen, you must be interviewed and trained.
    (E) As well as being eighteen, you must be interviewed and trained as well.

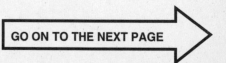

GO ON TO THE NEXT PAGE

42. In the context of the essay as a whole, which of the following is the best version of the underlined portion of sentence 13 (reproduced below)?

    But, soon, <u>my caseworker calls to tell</u> me that I had been assigned a little sister.

    (A) (As it is written now)
    (B) my caseworker is calling to tell
    (C) calling, my caseworker is telling
    (D) my caseworker had been calling to tell
    (E) my caseworker called to tell

43. Which of the following revisions of sentence 15 (reproduced below) would best improve the narrative flow of the last paragraph?

    I took the bus to her apartment.

    (A) The next morning, I took the bus to her apartment.
    (B) Taking the bus to her apartment, the new day was clear and beautiful.
    (C) While taking the bus to her apartment the next day, the idea struck me to go to the park.
    (D) I took the bus to her apartment, hoping to go to the park.
    (E) I was able to take the bus to her apartment.

44. The writer uses all of the following strategies in the passage EXCEPT

    (A) telling a story to make a point
    (B) making reference to other people's experiences
    (C) explaining a process
    (D) disputing conventional notions
    (E) making reference to the passage of time

GO ON TO THE NEXT PAGE

Questions 45-50. The following passage was written in response to an assignment to write an article for the school paper about a teacher's retirement.

(1) The retirement of Ms. Reingold is a loss to all in our school. (2) A dedicated individual, our school needs teachers like Ms. Reingold. (3) The school's idea to start a scholarship fund in Ms. Reingold's name is a wonderful one.

(4) It would be impossible to state all that Ms. Reingold has meant to us. (5) She began the "Students for a Better World" after school group almost twenty years ago. (6) It became one of the most popular and important extra curricular activities you could find. (7) And, club members were responsible for many of the changes around the school, such as the elimination of pesticide use in our district, the inclusion of the vegetarian meal for the school lunch and the campaign to raise money for cancer research. (8) Ms. Reingold taught us that we could work together, talk to companies and school officials. (9) Even though they didn't always listen, we felt that we had made the effort.

(10) In a time like this, it is easy to see how people can become cynical. (11) Ms. Reingold never did. (12) She always believed in us. (13) She put tremendous effort into the classes she taught. (14) She was also nationally recognized as a great teacher. (15) We learned from her both during school hours, in our committees and outside of them. (16) She was and still is an inspiration to all of us here at our school. (17) We should do things like this to commemorate our greatest teachers and leaders. (18) It may be a lot of work, but if our students work hard and they raise money, we can remember Ms. Reingold in the best way.

45. Which of the following is the best way to revise the underlined portion of sentence 2 (reproduced below)?

    A dedicated individual, <u>our school needs teachers like Ms. Reingold</u>.

    (A) our school is in need of teachers like Ms. Reingold
    (B) teachers like Ms. Reingold are just what our school needs
    (C) Ms. Reingold is the kind of teacher our school needs.
    (D) Ms. Reingold is just the kind we need as teachers in our school
    (E) need by our school is Ms. Reingold

46. Which of the following would be the best revision of the underlined portion of sentence 7 (reproduced below)?

    <u>*And, club members*</u> *were responsible for many of the changes around the school, such as the elimination of pesticide use in our district, the inclusion of the vegetarian meal for the school lunch and the campaign to raise money for cancer research.*

    (A) (as it is written)
    (B) Club members
    (C) Furthermore, club members
    (D) However, club members
    (E) Nevertheless, club members

47. Which of the following versions of sentence 15 (reproduced below) is the clearest?

    We learned from her both during school hours, in our committees and outside of them.

    (A) We learned from her both during school hours and outside of them, whether in our classes or our committees.
    (B) We learned both in our committees and in our classes and outside of our committees and classes.
    (C) Whether in committees or classes or out of them, we learned from her.
    (D) Whether we were in or out of them, committees or classes both, we learned from her.
    (E) Whether in school hours, in committees or out of, we learned from Ms. Reingold.

GO ON TO THE NEXT PAGE

48. The author could improve sentence 14 by

    (A) including an additional sentence with personal statistics about Ms. Reingold
    (B) including the author's personal opinion about Ms. Reingold
    (C) citing specific examples of national recognition
    (D) defining the word "great" more clearly
    (E) giving counterexamples

49. Which of the following replacements for the phrase "*do things like this*" in sentence 17 would make that sentence clearer?

    (A) raise money for things like scholarship funds
    (B) help people like Ms. Reingold
    (C) assist others
    (D) start committees after school
    (E) remember our finest

50. Which of the following versions of the underlined portion of sentence 18 (reproduced below) is best?

    It may be a lot of work, <u>but if our students work hard and they raise money</u>, we can remember Ms. Reingold in the best way.

    (A) (as it is written)
    (B) but if our students work hard and if they would raise money
    (C) however, if our students work hard and they would raise money
    (D) and if our students work hard and raise money
    (E) but if our students work hard and raise money

GO ON TO THE NEXT PAGE →

Directions: The following sentences test your knowledge of grammar, usage, word choice, and idiom.

Some sentences are correct.
No sentence contains more than one error.

You will find that the error, if there is one, is underlined and lettered. Elements of the sentence that are not underlined will not be changed. In choosing answers, follow the requirements of standard written English.

If there is an error, select the one underlined part that must be changed in order to make the sentence correct, and fill in the corresponding oval on your answer sheet.

If there is no error, fill in answer oval E.

EXAMPLE:

The other delegates and him immediately
A   B   C

accepted the resolution drafted by the
                                        D

neutral states. No error
                         E

SAMPLE ANSWER
Ⓐ ● Ⓒ Ⓓ Ⓔ

51. The head of our committee, Ms. Regine, had hoped
                    A
that our hard work will fund the new playground
     B   C
for our community. No error
     D   E

52. Cirrus clouds, those feathery, stringy clouds, are so
                        A   B
high up in the sky that they contain ice crystals.
          C   D
No error
E

53. Much of the information about mantas, such as how

it breeds, remains a mystery to the scientists who
A   B   C
study them. No error
      D   E

54. Now that school began this year, our class
                    A
feels excited about the prospect of hosting the
B   C
most successful senior fund raiser of all time.
        D
No error
E

55. Susan B. Anthony was one of the leaders
                        A
of the Suffragette movement, which focused for
        B   C   D
winning the right of women to vote. No error
                                        E

56. Preserving the Amazonian rain forest may seem
                                            A
unimportant to you and I, but doing so can affect
                      B   C
the future of our planet. No error
                D   E

GO ON TO THE NEXT PAGE

57. Either the president or, if <u>he is unable to serve</u>, the
                                        A

    vice president <u>are responsible</u> for <u>leading</u> the
                           B   C

    executive branch <u>of</u> our government. <u>No error</u>
                             D   E

58. As the philosophy of Socrates <u>is</u> so much more
                                          A

    famous <u>than his fellow Greek philosophers</u>, <u>it</u>
                              B   C

    shocks many people to learn <u>that he</u> never wrote a
                                          D

    book. <u>No error</u>
                 E

59. Before the 1800s, when cheap knives and forks

    <u>could be mass-produced</u> in factories, <u>most</u> people
                    A   B

    <u>ate</u> primarily using <u>their hands</u>. <u>No error</u>
       C   D   E

60. Jackson Pollack was famous for his huge canvasses

    and was helpful <u>to getting</u> the <u>wide</u> acceptance
                              A   B

    <u>of the art form</u> he <u>pioneered</u>, called Abstract
              C   D

    Expressionism. <u>No error</u>
                          E

END OF TEST

IF YOU FINISH BEFORE TIME IS CALLED, YOU MAY CHECK YOUR WORK ON EITHER PART OF THIS TEST.

HOW TO SCORE THE PRINCETON REVIEW
WRITING SUBJECT TEST

When you take the real exam, the proctors will collect your text booklet and bubble sheet and send your answer sheet to New Jersey where a computer (yes, a big, old-fashioned one that has been around since the '60s) looks at the pattern of filled-in ovals on your answer sheet and gives you a score. We couldn't include even a small computer with this book, so we are providing this more primitive way of scoring your exam.

DETERMINING YOUR SCORE

STEP 1 Using the answer key on the next page, determine how many questions you got right and how many you got wrong on the test. Remember, questions that you do not answer do not count as either right answers or wrong answers.

STEP 2 List the number of right answers here.

(A) _____

STEP 3 List the number of wrong answers here. Now divide that number by 4. (Use a calculator if you're feeling particularly lazy.)

(B) _____ ÷ 4 = (C) _____

STEP 4 Subtract the number of wrong answers divided by 4 from the number of correct answers. Round this score to the nearest whole number. This is your raw score.

(A) – (C) = _____

STEP 5 To determine your real score, take the number from Step 4 above and look it up in the left column of the Score Conversion Table on page 163; the corresponding score on the right is your score on the multiple-choice section of the exam.

ANSWER KEY TO SAT II WRITING DIAGNOSTIC TEST

1. E	16. C	31. B	46. B
2. C	17. B	32. C	47. A
3. D	18. C	33. C	48. C
4. C	19. E	34. B	49. A
5. E	20. B	35. A	50. E
6. A	21. C	36. A	51. C
7. A	22. C	37. D	52. E
8. A	23. B	38. E	53. A
9. E	24. D	39. B	54. A
10. D	25. B	40. D	55. D
11. A	26. D	41. D	56. B
12. D	27. A	42. E	57. B
13. A	28. C	43. A	58. B
14. D	29. E	44. D	59. E
15. B	30. D	45. C	60. A

SAT II WRITING TEST—SCORE CONVERSION TABLE

Recentered scale as of April 1995

Raw Score	College Board Scaled Score	Raw Score	College Board Scaled Score	Raw Score	College Board Scaled Score
60	600	35	460	10	320
59	600	34	450	09	310
58	600	33	450	08	310
57	590	32	440	07	300
56	580	31	440	06	300
55	580	30	430	05	290
54	570	29	430	04	280
53	570	28	420	03	280
52	560	27	410	02	270
51	550	26	410	01	270
50	550	25	400	00	260
49	540	24	400	−01	250
48	540	23	400	−02	250
47	530	22	390	−03	240
46	530	21	380	−04	240
45	520	20	380	−05	230
44	510	19	370	−06	230
43	510	18	370	−07	220
42	500	17	360	−08	210
41	500	16	350	−09	210
40	490	15	350	−10 through −15	200
39	480	14	340		
38	480	13	340		
37	470	12	330		
36	470	11	330		

Don't forget to add in your essay score! See page 79 for explanation.

PART ◆ V

The SAT II: Literature Test

10

Cracking the Literature Test

To crack the Literature Test, you need to do two things: First, become familiar with some basic literary terms; second, learn some techniques for analyzing a literary passage.

WHAT DOES THE SAT II: LITERATURE TEST TEST?

As with most standardized tests, especially those that are one hour long, the answer is "not much." It really would be impossible to test a broad range of topics in so short a time. As a result, the Literature Test, like the Writing Test, is relatively easy to prepare for.

You will be asked to interpret certain lines from literature. You will need to be familiar with some of the basic literary terms you've been tossing around in English classes all these years: Terms like "metaphor," "tone," and "imagery" will be covered; terms like "enjambment" and "metonymy" are far too obscure to be included on the exam. The last thing you should be doing at this point is sitting down with a reading list and a dictionary of literary terms. What you should be concentrating on is reviewing terms that sound vaguely familiar and pinning them down, and learning some great techniques for analyzing the types of passages that will be on the exam.

WHAT THE SAT II: LITERATURE TEST DOESN'T TEST

You don't need to know specific works of literature. This is really a test about reading comprehension.

The good news is you're not expected to be familiar with any works of literature. You won't be asked who the author is. You won't have to compare one piece with another. You won't have to identify the period from which a piece comes, so pack up your *Oxford Companion to English Literature.* This is a one-hour test of your ability to read and comprehend English literature. There isn't too much to know before you begin.

HOW THIS BOOK WORKS

This book is designed to give an overview of the information you will need to know to get a great score on the Literature SAT II. Each concept and term will be explained and there will be drills to help you understand how they work. We won't waste your time with lots of superfluous information.

HOW THE TEST IS STRUCTURED

The Literature Test consists of about sixty multiple-choice questions based on six to eight reading passages. The passages come mainly from English literature (slightly more than half) and American literature (slightly less than half). Occasionally, some literature from other cultures will crop up, but it will be text that was originally written in English—no translations of poems by Verlaine. The test is also split fairly evenly into passages from different time periods.

Expect roughly:

The Literature Test is made up of six to eight passages. Most of these passages come from either English or American literature.

- one-third from Renaissance and seventeenth-century literature

- one-third from eighteenth- and nineteenth-century literature

- one-third from twentieth-century literature

Again, you will not be asked to identify the source of a passage. However, it may be useful in the context of a question to recognize something as modern or classic.

The passages will also be broken up by their style. There will be about:

- two to four passages of prose
- two to four passages of poetry
- one passage from drama or a miscellaneous style

Each passage will be followed by five to ten questions.

Some books will give you reading lists. Although having read literature before you take this test will certainly help you, this is not the time to sit down and start plowing through *Pride and Prejudice*. Save that for your vacation.

Each passage has five to ten questions.

How Do I Know If I Should Take the Literature Test?

If you're unsure about this, contact the college you will probably be applying to or start perusing college catalogs. Generally, colleges that require SAT II Subject Tests require you to take three. If any one is required, it is usually the Writing Test. Many schools strongly recommend math.

After that, you may choose any other tests you want. Your number one concern is to determine which tests you will score well on. Then you will want to think about the purposes for which the test will be used. Some colleges will use them to exempt you from requirements. Others will use them to evaluate you. So, if you plan to be a bio major, take the Biology Test. If you plan to be an English major, take the Writing and Literature tests. If you're a whiz at *anything*, take that test.

So, first check your requirements.

Second, assess your needs.

Then review and take a diagnostic test like the one at the end of the review section and determine whether this is the test for you.

Check with the schools and see which Subject Tests, if any, are required. Beyond that, ask yourself which tests you think you can score well on.

How the Test Is Scored

The Literature Test is scored like the Writing Test, all the other SAT II: Subject Tests, and the SAT I. You will get a raw score based on the following equation:

$$\text{number right} - \frac{1}{4}(\text{number wrong}) = \text{raw score}$$

In other words, you get a point for every right answer and lose a quarter of a point for every wrong answer. For the most part, every raw point translates to approximately ten points in the scaled score. The resulting scaled score will be in that old familiar 200–800 index.

For each correct answer, you receive 1 point. For each incorrect answer, you lose $\frac{1}{4}$ point.

The Two Important Things to Remember

ANYTIME YOU CAN ELIMINATE EVEN ONE
WRONG ANSWER, YOU MUST GUESS.

If it makes you feel any better, say "take educated guesses." There, that sounds perfectly reasonable, doesn't it? Let's review some of the math (MATH?) involved in scoring the test and see if you can't be convinced to blacken in those ovals a little more frequently than you may have in the past.

If you decide to take, let's say, an hour-long nap during the English Lit Test, rising only to hear the old five-minute warning from your warm and caring proctor, you'd probably fill in the same letter all the way down and take your chances, right? Now, in a statistically perfect world, you'd probably get about one out of every five questions right. Five answer choices, randomly filled in, should yield about that result. Check it out:

Out of sixty questions:

$$12 \text{ right} = 12 \times 1 = 12$$

$$48 \text{ wrong} = \frac{1}{4} \times 48 = 12$$

$$12 - 12 = 0$$

Those fun-loving folks at ETS have achieved their goal, and you nappers got a score of 200 on the test. The point is, you're not actually penalized for random guesses, it's just that *nothing happens if you guess*—an important distinction. Look what happens to our educated guesser:

If you eliminate even one obviously wrong answer per question, you now have a one in four chance of getting the answer right.

So, if you get one right, you gain a point. If you get three wrong, you lose $\frac{3}{4}$ of a point and your net gain is $\frac{1}{4}$ of a point. Doesn't seem like much? Remember, one raw point will get you about ten points in a converted score—nothing to scoff at (if you are the scoffing type, that is).

Listen, even if you don't understand any of this math stuff, it doesn't matter. As long as you absorb the one important fact that ANYTIME YOU CAN ELIMINATE EVEN *ONE* WRONG ANSWER, YOU MUST GUESS. We mean it. This is a very important rule to remember. (If you're taking the Writing Test as well, you already know this rule.)

DON'T RUSH!

You see, you don't need to finish every question to get a great score on this test. Don't be afraid to skip a few questions as you go. Most important, pace yourself. Don't linger on any question too long. ETS isn't going to give you any extra points for hard questions, so why should you spend more time on them? Either skip them completely or get rid of a couple of wrong answers and make the best guess you can. Since the questions are not in order of difficulty, you will have to determine for yourself which questions look too hard. Be completely subjective and one-sided—skip a question if you don't like the looks of it. Check out this pacing chart:

Remember, you must guess if you can eliminate even one wrong answer. One raw-score point can give you approximately ten scaled-score points.

Accuracy is more important than speed, so slow down. You can still get a good score without answering every question on the test.

You can:

Leave 10 blank	get 4 wrong	and still get a 650
Leave 10 blank	get 8 wrong	and still get a 600
Leave 15 blank	get 10 wrong	and still get a 550
Leave 20 blank	get 10 wrong	and still get a 500

So, *slow down*, *guess more aggressively*, and most important of all:

DON'T PANIC.

You are taking the test, the test is not taking you. You've got sixty minutes to take this exam. So don't waste time on a passage you hate and never get to a really great passage you would have loved to do. Keep track of the types of passages you like best and on which you tend to score highest. If poetry is your weak point and a poem is the first thing on the exam, save it for later. The first thing you want to do is find a selection that you feel comfortable with. You'll get that all-important boost of confidence right away. Sixty minutes is not a long time. Try to hit your stride in the first five minutes, not at the halfway point.

When you've decided the order in which you will do the passages, decide question order as well. There's no law that says you must go in order. Skip the Roman numeral I, II, and III questions until later. If one has a word you've never seen, come back to it. Don't get psyched out before you get going. Nothing feels better than getting questions right at the start. Then, if you don't get something three quarters through the test—no sweat. You're allowed to skip some anyway.

CRACKING THE LITERATURE TEST: PART TWO

Okay, there's all this talk of guessing and pacing and moving and not panicking; now let's talk about how exactly you're going to do this. Before we get into the specifics of the test, there are some general test-taking techniques that can be used nicely on the Literature Test.

MEET JOE BLOGGS

Joe Bloggs is your average, everyday high school test taker. He gets pretty good grades in school. He also consistently gets those average test scores you hear so much about. Why? Well, Joe cruises through most of the exam, but he's got one fatal flaw when he gets to a tricky question—he believes in the basic goodness of every person. He believes that the fine, upstanding people at ETS wouldn't trick him. So, rather than look out for trick answers on hard questions, Joe will pick the obvious ones over and over. And lose points. But you, savvy test taker that you will become, will start to recognize a "Joe Bloggs" answer on a hard question and you will avoid it like the plague.

Do the passages in the order you want to do them.

Do the questions for a passage in the order you want to do them.

Joe Bloggs is your average test taker.

On a hard question, Joe always picks an easy answer —and that's why Joe *always* misses hard questions.

Check out this actual question from the Literature Test:

24. As it is used in the passage, the word "impertinent" (line 22) means

    (A) distressing
    (B) rude
    (C) exaggerated
    (D) critical
    (E) irrelevant

Now, which of these responses would Joe, who probably isn't thinking about the word in context, pick? Chances are he'd go for (B). Remember this: On a "words in context question," the obvious straightforward definition of a word will be wrong. It wouldn't be that obvious. If this were a vocabulary test, you could rely on definitions. Joe forgot that this is the Literature Test, and words in context are going to have slightly different meanings. The choice here happens to be (E). "Rude" was the first definition of the word. "Irrelevant" was the secondary or "never used by most people" definition of "impertinent."

LINE REFERENCE QUESTIONS

Don't just read the line reference ETS gives you. Read the surrounding lines as well.

Many questions on the Literature Test will ask you to go back to a specific line to find a word or a phrase. In any line reference question, always read a couple of lines before and a couple of lines after the actual reference. Remember, when Joe is asked to go to line 14, he looks only at line 14. Since so much of this test has to do with interpretation *in context*, the answer will probably be more *around* line 14 than in it.

So, as far as Joe Bloggs is concerned, watch out for an answer choice that appears to be too obvious. This is not to say that your instincts will never be correct. Most of the time they will. But if the question looks a little difficult, don't shy away from the less obvious response. Joe hates those answers. He hates to pick words he doesn't recognize. Sometimes an obscure word makes the best guess. If you're unsure, go with an answer that's off the beaten track.

SPECIAL TECHNIQUES FOR SPECIAL QUESTION TYPES

A hard question usually has a hard answer.

Questions on the Literature Test fall into three categories:

1. plain old multiple-choice questions

2. Roman numeral I, II, and III questions

3. EXCEPT/NOT questions

The last two types are a little strange, so they merit different treatments. You may be familiar with these question types if you've already taken the SAT I.

ROMAN NUMERAL I, II, AND III QUESTIONS

These can be especially tricky because instead of simply finding the right answer, you must decide if more than one possible choice may be correct. Look at an example:

The author intends for the little boy to function as

   I. a representative of a particular age group
  II. a symbol of powerlessness
 III. a sympathetic figure

(A) I only
(B) II only
(C) I and III only
(D) II and III only
(E) I, II, and III

Once you know one statement in a Roman numeral question is true or false, go to your answer choices and start eliminating.

Go through your options one by one. It's not a bad idea to begin with the Roman numeral that appears most frequently. So, here, start with I. If you decide that I is incorrect, you can eliminate all choices that contain I. Now, you eliminate (A), (C), and (E). Since answer choices (B) and (D) are the only two remaining, and they both contain Roman numeral II, you can be sure that II is right. You only need to check Roman numeral III. If you had decided that Roman numeral I was right, which choices would you eliminate?—(B) and (D), the only choices that do *not* contain I. Go through these systematically and you will avoid not only careless errors, but also extra work. Practice this technique until you are comfortable with it.

EXCEPT/NOT QUESTIONS

These can be diabolical. Typical questions read like this:

> All of the following are devices used in the
> selection EXCEPT:

or:

> Which of the following is NOT suggested in the
> above poem?

The problem is that it's very easy to forget, by the time you're at choice (D), that you were looking for something that *wasn't* in the poem, instead of something that *was*. You can avoid careless errors by (1) circling the word *EXCEPT* or *NOT*, even if it is in capital letters, and (2) writing a *Y* for yes if the answer is true, or an *N* for no if the answer is false, next to each answer choice. Seeing four *Y*s and one *N* should remind you that this is an EXCEPT/NOT question.

Play the "yes/no" game for EXCEPT/NOT questions.

> All of the following are true of lines 23–27
> EXCEPT:
>
> Y   (A) It contains a metaphor
> Y   (B) It has a regular rhythm
> Y   (C) It evokes a strong image
> N   (D) It represents a change in meter
> Y   (E) It is evocative

Hence, (D) is the answer. Again, practice the technique.

BEFORE YOU BEGIN ANSWERING QUESTIONS, HOWEVER...

Take a look at the passages. Decide the order *you* want to do them in. How to decide? As you practice, see which types of passages you are strongest in: poetry, prose, or drama. Look for a passage that interests you.

Once you've ordered the section, take a minute to read through the passage before you tackle its questions. Don't spend too much time reading; you just want to understand the general idea. Then tackle the questions that deal with specific lines or words. Go back and reread the reference, *and* a few lines above it and below it. Once you've done all of those you will be best able to answer questions dealing with the passage's tone or voice.

Don't forget about pacing.

A FINAL NOTE

The above techniques are just that—techniques. They are not facts to be memorized, but ways of doing something. As such, you should be comfortable and familiar with them on the day of the test. Just as you will be familiar with the directions, the format, and the content of the exam, you will want to be familiar with the way you plan to take the test. Know when to skip. Know the order in which you'll do the test. Be familiar with the pacing chart. Decide in advance about how many questions you'd like to leave out. And practice the techniques.

11
Literary Terms

INTRODUCTION TO ANALYZING POETRY, PROSE, AND DRAMA

As discussed before, the Literature Test doesn't review your knowledge of literature in general. But there are some terms it would be helpful to know. To begin, let's define the following categories:

Passages on the Literature Test will be poetry, prose, or drama.

POETRY: A poem is a *rhythmic* expression of feeling or ideas, kind of like the lyrics to a song. It may rhyme, or it may not.

PROSE: This one's easy—if it's not poetry, it's prose. Prose is generally broken into two categories: fiction and nonfiction.

DRAMA: A play; something that is intended to be acted out. Plays can be written in verse or in a more conversational style.

LITERARY TERMS YOU NEED TO KNOW

Become familiar with the basic literary terms listed below.

Here's a list of the basics. Each is followed by examples or a discussion of what it is. If you're familiar with the term, move on. Concentrate on any that are unfamiliar to you or that you feel you could use some work in.

ALLEGORY: A story with underlying symbols that really represent something else. A character can be allegorical.

Example:

> The nursery rhyme "Humpty Dumpty" was really a political allegory, representing people in government who were falling from power.

ALLITERATION: The use of a repeated consonant sound, usually at the beginning of a series of words.

Examples:

> Silently *s*talking about the corridor . . .

> Falling, *f*alling, *f*earfully *f*alling . . .

ALLUSION: A reference to something or someone, usually literary.

Example:

> Mr. Jones got the neighborhood kids to do his yard work—just as Tom Sawyer got the kids to paint the fence.

ANACHRONISM: Placing a person in an inappropriate historical situation. It can be deliberate or unintentional.

Example:

> George Washington rode his limousine downtown for the inauguration.

ANALOGY: Comparing something to something else.

> Example:

> > Starting a new job is like starting a new school year.

ANTAGONIST: The major character opposing the protagonist, usually the villain.

> Example:

> > Boris Badanov, Bullwinkle's enemy, is my favorite antagonist.

ANTHROPOMORPHISM: Assigning human attributes such as emotions or physical characteristics to nonhuman things. Used almost exclusively for attributing human characteristics to animals.

> Examples:

> > My cat, Fluffy, is always so happy to see me.

> > The mother rhinoceros was depressed for weeks over the loss of her offspring to the cruel hunter.

DICTION: Choice of words. Diction can be incorrect if the wrong word is used. It can be stilted or flowery. It can set the tone.

> Examples:

> > **Incorrect diction:** *Your* going to be sorry you didn't study.

> > (Should be *You're*)

> > **Stilted diction:** "One should always remind oneself to take extra money when one is going shopping."

Choice of words can be important. Wrong words can be used to indicate a character's ignorance or humor. Flowery words can reveal a character's pretension.

FABLE: A story that has a moral, usually involving animals as the main characters.

> Example:

> > Aesop's fable about the grasshopper and the ant is a great illustration of why you should work hard and prepare for bad times.

HYPERBOLE: A deliberate exaggeration.

> Examples:

> > Taking that test was the easiest thing I've ever done.

> > There were a billion people at the concert.

I'm going to be grounded for about ten years when my parents find out where I was last night.

The new teacher gave us about fifty hours of homework for tonight.

IRONY: An expression of meaning that is the opposite of the literal meaning.

Example:

The music is *so loud* that I can hardly hear it.

Stories can be ironic as well, when they end up in a way that is the opposite of what you would have expected. A story about an obsessively clean man who is killed by a garbage truck is ironic. O. Henry's classic story "The Gift of the Magi" is a great example of irony. The husband sells his watch to buy his wife a Christmas present of an ornate hair comb, only to find that she sold her hair to buy him a watch chain.

METAPHOR: A metaphor is a comparison like a simile, but it doesn't use the words *like* or *as*. It's a little more subtle.

It's important to note, however, that in literary criticism, the word *metaphor* is frequently used when, strictly speaking, the term *simile* applies. Don't be confused if you are asked if the writer is using metaphor and you see the words *like* or *as*.

Examples:

She was a breath of fresh air in the classroom.

The new principal was stricter than a prison warden.

Johnny is a tiger when it comes to football.

ONOMATOPOEIA: A word intended to simulate the actual sound of the thing or action it describes.

Examples:

A *buzzing* bee.

"*Bam!*" The superhero hit the criminal.

The snake *hissed* at its predator.

OXYMORON: A phrase in which the words are contradictory.

Examples:

He was happy in his pessimism.

They were intelligently ignorant.

Sometimes an oxymoron is used for comic effect; sometimes it is used to illustrate a paradox.

PARABLE: A story that has a moral.

> Example:

> > The story of the good Samaritan is a famous parable from the Bible.

PARADOX: This is a phrase that appears to be contradictory, but which actually contains some basic truth that resolves the apparent contradiction.

> Example:

> > Although he was sentenced to ten years of hard labor, the guilt-ridden criminal looked as though a weight had been lifted from his shoulders.

PATHOS: Something that evokes a feeling of pity or sympathy. Think of the word *pathetic*. A pathetic person is an element of pathos in a story.

> Example:

> > And so, the little orphan girl curled up on the cold steps of the church and tried to sleep.

PERSONIFICATION: Assigning human attributes to something nonhuman.

> Examples:

> > I hope that fortune will smile on me when I take my exam.

> > My car always seems so miserable when I let someone else drive.

PROTAGONIST: The main character, usually the hero.

> Example:

> > Jane Eyre, Charlotte Brontë's most famous protagonist, is my favorite heroine in English literature.

SATIRE: Ridicule of a subject.

> Example:

> > *Saturday Night Live* often makes use of satire. When the cast pokes fun at the president, they are *satirizing* the politics of the country.

Satire is humorous and often intended to point out something to us about what is usually a serious subject.

SIMILE: A simile is a comparison of two unlike things using either the word *like* or the word *as*.

Examples:

> I'm as quick as a cricket.
>
> He's as sly as a fox.
>
> She was greeted like a rooster in a hen house.

Similes can be evocative of a mood or a spirit. They are frequently used in poetry to evoke an idea through an image.

DRILL # 1

Try your hand at recognizing the following.

If you see a metaphor, mark the space with an *M*.

If you see a simile, mark the space with an *S*.

If you see personification, mark the space with a *P*.

If you see anthropomorphism, mark the space with an *A*.

_____ 1. She moved through the room like a cool summer breeze.

_____ 2. The house shivered in the cold winter wind.

_____ 3. Marie was as sad as a basset hound when she heard the news.

_____ 4. The news that she had won the sweepstakes was a dream come true to Mary Anne.

_____ 5. Bunnies often feel dejected when kept in their hutches for too long.

_____ 6. The wind sang a song of melancholy as it whistled through the field.

_____ 7. Taking standardized tests is torture unless you're prepared.

_____ 8. Like a soldier marching into battle, the student body president went to meet with the new principal.

_____ 9. That test was no day at the beach.

_____10. My puppy is too proud to wear a silly collar like that one!

You can check your answers on page 217.

Drill # 2

If the sentence contains onomatopoeia, mark it with an *O*.

If the sentence contains alliteration, mark it with an *A*.

If the sentence contains an oxymoron, mark it with an *OX*.

If the sentence contains an anachronism, mark it with an *AN*.

_____ 1. Driving a tank into battle, George Washington assaulted the British and won the war.

_____ 2. The hissing of the snake alerted the hikers to the possible danger within the cave.

_____ 3. He was conspicuous by his absence at the new student meeting.

_____ 4. Sailing swiftly through the water, they won the race.

_____ 5. Napoleon was a giant in his smallness.

_____ 6. Shakespeare tapped out plays on his own word processor.

_____ 7. "Knock, knock, knock" was tapped out to signal that a club member was at the door.

_____ 8. The new attorney on the case was practically pompous.

_____ 9. The situation with the new smoking policy became perfectly chaotic.

_____ 10. "Hoo, Hoo," called the owl, sending chills up our spines.

You can check your answers on page 217.

DRILL # 3

Read the following plot synopses.

Mark *A* if the story sounds like an allegory.

Mark *S* if it sounds like a satire.

Mark *P* if it sounds like a parable.

Mark *F* if it sounds like a fable.

_____ 1. The story was told, long ago, of a rich man who gave away all his money after realizing that it brought him no pleasure. He found out, only after living as a pauper, who his real friends were.

_____ 2. The fictitious land of Munchkinville is taken over by a bunch of greedy giants. They claim that they will take care of the less fortunate, but they only steal money from the poor and use it to live the high life.

_____ 3. The proud cat lingered on her comfortable pillow all day long, purring contentedly. She never once helped with the work the other animals did for the farm. She wouldn't even catch mice. "You're too lazy," the other animals chided. Little did she know how right they would turn out to be.

_____ 4. The bumbling political candidates arrived one morning for breakfast at the Knights of Columbus. None knew the others would be there. The ensuing fight over who would sit at the head of the table was fitting for ten-year-olds.

You can check your answers on page 217.

12

Analyzing Poetry

In the last chapter, you learned that poetry is simply a rhythmic expression of feelings and ideas. That's a pretty vague definition. And if you've ever studied or read any poetry at all, you're certainly aware that it encompasses a very broad range of material. This is a category that ranges from the works of William Shakespeare to those of Maya Angelou and beyond. Some people include lyrics from songs as poetry.

As far as what makes good poetry or bad poetry, that's another story. Classic poetry typically has a very formal, rigid structure, as in this poem from the seventeenth century:

> "A Pilgrim's Solace"
>
> Stay, O sweet, and do not rise!
> The light that shines comes from thine eyes;
> The day breaks not: it is my heart,
> Because that you and I must part.
>   Stay! or else my joys will die
>   And perish in their infancy.

This anonymous poem was written in 1612, when the rules of poetry were very elaborate. This poem has a certain rhyme scheme—the scheme tells you which lines rhyme with which other lines. The rhyme scheme here would be: A A B B C C. This means that the first line rhymes with the second line, the third line rhymes with the fourth line, and the fifth and sixth lines rhyme.

There are lots of different standard rhyme schemes, and it's worth noting only that they exist. You won't be tested on rhyme schemes.

The next thing to note is that the poem has a certain meter. That's the beat of the line—like reggae or rap. As with the rhyme scheme, there is often a rigid pattern to the meter of the lines. We could get into a whole discussion here of iambic pentameter or dactylic tetrameter, but what would be the point? What you should be aware of is that there is a rhythm and a rhyme. In classic poetry it was very strictly adhered to, much as musical forms were strictly adhered to. If you take classical music lessons, you know that there are sonatas, fugues, and symphonies, and that each of these terms represents a specific form. In poetry there are sonnets, quatrains, and epic poems, and each is a specific form.

So whenever you see deliberate rhyme schemes or rhythms, you're probably reading classic poetry. This would also indicate to you that the poet is dealing with classic themes.

WHAT ARE CLASSIC THEMES?

Well, it would be strange to read a Shakespearean sonnet that was about urban crime or racial division. These were not hot topics in those days. Classic themes more frequently ran along the lines of love, love lost, beauty, and death. Metaphors stood for your lover, or for death, or for truth. The themes were universal and general. Some addressed political issues of the day.

It's useful to categorize a poem as classical because it gives you a framework within which to work.

Classic poetry tends to have a formal, rigid structure.

Classic poetry tends to have deliberate rhyme schemes.

Classic poetry often has themes involving love, beauty, and death.

POETRY BECOMES MODERN

Just as music grew from formal sonatas to a wider range of forms, so poetry grew from sonnets to free and blank verse. You should be familiar with these two terms:

> **FREE VERSE** is a poem without regular meter or line length.
>
> **BLANK VERSE** is a poem with a regular meter, but unrhymed.

Modern poetry tends to use free or blank verse.

These are favorite forms for modern poets. Let's take a look at some modern poetry.

The following poem is by Langston Hughes:

"Brass spittoons"

Clean the spittoons, boy.
Detroit,
Chicago,
Atlantic City,
(5) Palm Beach.
Clean the spittoons.
The steam in hotel kitchens,
And the smoke in hotel lobbies,
And the slime in hotel spittoons:
(10) Part of my life.

Hey, boy!
A nickel,
A dime,
A dollar,
(15) Two dollars a day.
Hey boy!
A nickel,
A dime,
A dollar,
(20) Two dollars
Buys shoes for the baby.
House rent to pay.
God on Sunday.
My God!

(25) Babies and church
and women and Sunday
all mixed up with dimes and
dollars and clean spittoons
and house rent to pay.
(30) Hey, boy!

A bright bowl of brass is beautiful to the Lord.
Bright polished brass like the cymbals

Of King David's dancers,
Like the wine cups of Solomon.
(35)   Hey, boy!
A clean spittoon on the altar of the Lord.
A clean bright spittoon all newly polished, —
At least I can offer that.
Com'mere boy!

This is an example of free verse. The meter varies from place to place and is dictated by the content instead of by the form. Hughes is able to evoke a feeling with the way the poem moves, in addition to the words it uses. Good poetry, just like good song lyrics, moves effortlessly, either with a rhyme scheme or without. Things like meter and rhyme, or lack thereof, should never be too obvious. Don't you just hate when you're listening to a great song and a stupid word pops out because the songwriter was obviously trying to rhyme? Or a whole phrase sticks out because it was not matched to the rest of the song in beat or rhyme?

Poets, whether modern or classical, face the challenge of using form to their advantage.

ANALYZING THE POEMS

Look back at the seventeenth-century poem. See if you can find some of the literary techniques you learned in the previous chapter. It's not a very long poem, but see how much you can dig out of it. You'll find an answer key on page 217.

Try to think of a poem in terms of the basic literary terms you've learned.

What is the analogy he makes?

_____

_____

_____

Where is the example of personification?

_____

_____

_____

Where does he use alliteration?

_____

_____

_____

Another line of personification?

_____

_____

_____

Take a look at what you've just written. You've found all these great examples of personification and alliteration and analogy. Now think.

What is the overall effect of these techniques?

Jot down some ideas as to what the main idea of the poem is. What is the poet trying to communicate? Does he do it effectively?

_____

_____

_____

Now, examine Hughes's poem. There's a lot more text to look at, and we should find more devices. Again, answers are on page 217.

Where does Hughes use alliteration?

_____

_____

Where do you see an example of personification?

_____

_____

Another example of alliteration?

_____

_____

Where does he use allusion?

_____

_____

Where does he use metaphor?

_____

_____

_____

What's the overall effect of the poem? Does the use of these devices enhance that effect? What's Hughes trying to communicate? Why do you think he uses the words he does to express these ideas?

_____

_____

_____

Let's look at another poem.

This time, try to analyze it without knowing who wrote it, or when it was written. Check your answers on page 217.

"There Is No Frigate Like a Book"

There is no frigate like a book
    To take us lands away,
Nor any coursers like a page
    Of prancing poetry.
(5)   This traverse may the poorest take
    Without oppress of toll;
How frugal is the chariot
    That bears a human soul!

Where is there a simile?

_____

_____

_____

Another simile?

_____

_____

Where is there a metaphor?

_____

_____

_____

Another metaphor?

_____

_____

_____

What is the effect of the metaphors and similes used?

_____

_____

_____

What do you think the main idea of the poem is?

_____

_____

_____

By the way, that poem was written by Emily Dickinson, who lived from 1830 to 1886. Her simple poems are filled with imagery.

Now, analyze the following poem.

"The Dying Christian To His Soul"

Vital spark of heav'nly flame!
Quit, O quit this mortal frame:
Trembling, hoping, ling'ring, flying,
O the pain, the bliss of dying!
(5) Cease, fond Nature, cease thy strife,
And let me languish into life.

Hark! they whisper; angels say,
Sister Spirit, come away!
(10) What is this absorbs me quite?
Steals my senses, shuts my sight,
Drowns my spirits, draws my breath?
Tell me, my soul, can this be death?

The world recedes; it disappears!
(15) Heav'n opens on my eyes! my ears
With sounds seraphic ring!
Lend, lend your wings! I mount! I fly!
    O Grave! where is thy victory?
    O Death! where is thy sting?

Analyze the mystery poem, then check your answers on page 217:

Where does the author use personification?

_____

_____

_____

Where does the author use alliteration?

_____

_____

_____

Where is there another example of alliteration?

_____

_____

_____

Personification, again?

_____

_____

_____

What is the effect of the meter? Is it rapid or slow?

_____

_____

_____

What is the effect of the punctuation?

_____

_____

_____

How do the different elements work together to create a mood? Does the overall effect complement the subject matter?

_____

_____

_____

Does this strike you as a modern or classic poem?

_____

_____

_____

The poem is by Alexander Pope (1688–1744).

A Final Note on Analyzing Poetry

As you may have noticed, the literary devices help to define the poem. It is not a bad idea to do all the specific questions on a poem, to decipher the meanings of certain phrases before you tackle the main idea question, if there is one. Often, it becomes clear after you break a poem apart what the whole was intended to mean.

Let's try one poem, with questions:

> "Madman's Song"
>
> Better to see your cheek grown hollow,
> Better to see your temple worn,
> Than to forget to follow, follow,
> After the sound of a silver horn.
>
> (5) Better to bind your brow with willow
> And follow, follow until you die,
> Than to sleep with your head on a golden pillow,
> Nor lift it up when the hunt goes by.
>
> Better to see your cheek grown sallow
> (10) And your hair grown gray, so soon, so soon,
> Than to forget to hallo, hallo,
> After the milk-white hounds of the moon.
> —*Elinor Wylie*

Try doing the specific questions for a poetry passage before tackling the main idea question.

1. What is the effect of using "silver" to describe the "horn" (line 4)?

    (A) To imply that the horn is not as valuable as a golden horn
    (B) To foreshadow any item that may be used in the "hunt" (line 8)
    (C) To be alliterative with the word *sound*
    (D) To indicate that the image would be bright
    (E) To symbolize the beauty of wealth

2. Given in context, the word "hallo" (line 11) is probably meant to convey which of the following?

    (A) a form of greeting
    (B) another form of the word "hollow" (line 1)
    (C) an echo
    (D) a sound like the hounds might make baying at the moon
    (E) a variation on the word "halo"

3. The attitude of the author toward the reader is best described as

   (A) openly hostile
   (B) gently insistent
   (C) didactic
   (D) ambivalent
   (E) disgusted

4. The author is most probably addressing the poem to

   (A) someone who has lost touch with what is important
   (B) someone who is ashamed of her background
   (C) someone who has become very wealthy
   (D) someone who is about to die
   (E) someone who is vain

5. In this poem, the images are meant to convey which of the following?

   I. Someone who has been committed to an insane asylum
   II. Someone who has lost passion for life
   III. Someone who has been filled with passion

   (A) I only
   (B) II only
   (C) II and III only
   (D) III only
   (E) I, II, and III

Check your answers on page 218.

13

Analyzing Prose

Prose can be either fiction or nonfiction.

Let's go back to the first definition of prose that was put forth a couple of chapters ago: Prose is anything that is not poetry. Well, of course, you don't really like definitions of things that tell what they *aren't* instead of what they *are*, so let's talk about what prose *is*.

Prose is the way you speak every day. If someone followed you around and reported on your actions and conversations, the result would be prose. Creepy prose, no doubt, but let's not dwell on someone following you around all day.

Prose can be divided into two rough categories: fiction and nonfiction. Fiction is made up and nonfiction is pretty much true.

ANALYZING FICTION

An amazing number of elements go into making a work of fiction. Just as in good poetry, where the beat and meter blend with the subject, in good fiction the elements blend together seamlessly.

Fiction tells a story. It involves characters, plots, and themes.

Some of the elements at work in fiction are characters, plots, and themes. All of these things work together to tell a story. The purpose of the work of fiction can vary from simple entertainment or teaching a moral lesson to revealing something great and true about humankind.

THE DIFFERENT TYPES OF FICTION

Probably the most familiar form of fiction is the novel. The novel as a form has been around for about six hundred years. It's hard to even imagine what life would be like without novels. A novel is just an extended story. A novella is simply a short novel.

Novels can be categorized by *genre*. The genre is the type of fiction. Some genres are:

Genre is the type of fiction, such as mystery, romance, and historical.

- ◆ mystery or detective novels

- ◆ romance novels

- ◆ realistic fiction

- ◆ historical fiction

- ◆ humorous fiction

You may have noticed, browsing around bookstores or libraries, that books are often separated by genre. The reason for this is that certain genres are extremely popular with certain people. People often tend to like one sort of book, and they'll read anything in that category. Genre fiction can be popular for writers as well. Often, they follow a specific formula and can write lots of books in one genre.

CHARACTERS IN NOVELS

The protagonist, or the hero, is usually a sympathetic figure.

Probably one of the main reasons people read novels is to meet new and interesting characters. Characters work in a story in a lot of different ways. The protagonist, as you remember from the definitions, is the hero or heroine of the story. Most of the time, the protagonist is a sympathetic character. In other words, he or she is someone you can relate to; someone whose problems you can understand or you would want to understand. If a character is not sympathetic at all, the novel may not be compelling enough to read. Think back on some of the books you may have read through the years. How much could you sympathize with the plights of the protagonists?

In *The Color Purple*, by Alice Walker, the protagonist, Celie, has problems that you may not be able to imagine. But her strength and courage make readers want her to survive. Her character makes the book memorable; it drives the story, and gets the reader to turn the page.

Jane Eyre, Charlotte Brontë's great novel, presents one of the most compelling figures in English fiction. The reader follows her from her youth through womanhood. Knowing about a person makes that character more interesting to read about, and more sympathetic.

As you can see, characters are incredibly important to a novel. If a character represents a certain kind of person, he or she is said to be an *archetype*. Felix Unger of *The Odd Couple* was an archetypal neat person. If a character doesn't really possess the qualities of courage and idealism, he or she is said to be an *antihero*. Sometimes antiheroes can be even more interesting because they've got faults like the rest of us. Modern novels have frequently centered around the antihero—someone who succeeds in spite of his or her flaws.

THE USE OF VOICE

Fiction can be written in three different voices. They are:

THE FIRST PERSON: This is when the narrator is the main character in the story. It is easy to recognize because it uses the pronoun "I" in the narrative (not dialogue) part.

Read this example from the opening lines of one of the great classics, *Moby-Dick* by Herman Melville.

> Call me Ishmael. Some years ago—never mind how long precisely—having little or no money in my purse, and nothing particular to interest me on shore, I thought I would sail about a little and see the watery part of the world. It is a way I have of driving off the spleen, and regulating the circulation. Whenever I find myself growing grim about the mouth; whenever it is a damp, drizzly November in my soul; whenever I find myself involuntarily pausing before coffin warehouses, and bringing up the rear of every funeral I meet; and especially whenever my hypos get such an upper hand of me, that it requires a strong moral principle to prevent me from deliberately stepping into the street, and methodically knocking people's hats off—then, I account it high time to get to sea as soon as I can.

A character who represents a certain kind of person is said to be an archetype.

The antihero is often more interesting than the hero because the antihero has flaws.

A first-person narrative uses the pronoun "I." This voice is very personal and revealing.

Now answer these questions (you can check your answers on page 218):

What is the effect of the use of first person?

_____

_____

_____

Where is the metaphor? What is the effect of using a metaphor?

_____

_____

_____

What is your impression of the narrator?

_____

_____

_____

Would the impression be the same had the author used third person? Why or why not?

_____

_____

_____

The first person voice here immediately sets up a dialogue between the reader and the narrator. This is going to be *his* story. It is an intensely personal narrative, revealing much about the person we have yet to meet.

A second-person narrative uses the pronoun "you." This voice tries to make the reader a character in the story rather than just an observer.

SECOND PERSON: This is when the narrator speaks using the pronoun "you." It is the least common of voices, although some recent modern novels have been quite successful with it. The second person is often used to create a special relationship between the reader and the work. By using "you," the author in effect makes the reader a character in the book, rather than just an observer. *If on a winter's night a traveler* by Italo Calvino is an example of a novel written largely in the second person. Here's a passage:

A key turns in the lock. You fall silent, as if you wanted to surprise her, as if to confirm to yourself and to her that your being here is something natural. But the footstep is not hers. Slowly a man materializes in the hall, you see his shadow through the curtains, a leather windbreaker, a step indicating familiarity with the place but hesitant, as if someone is looking for something. You recognize him. It is Irnerio.

THIRD PERSON: Here the narrator speaks using the third person pronouns "him," "her," "he," "she," "them," and "they."

Look at a selection from the John Steinbeck work *Of Mice and Men:*

> They had walked in single file down the path, and even in the open one stayed behind the other. Both were dressed in denim trousers and in denim coats with brass buttons. Both wore black, shapeless hats and both carried tight blanket rolls slung over their shoulders. The first man was small and quick, dark of face, with restless eyes and sharp, strong features. Every part of him was defined: small, strong hands, slender arms, a thin and bony nose. Behind him walked his opposite, a huge man, shapeless of face, with large, pale eyes, with wide, sloping shoulders; and he walked heavily, dragging his feet a little, the way a bear drags his paws. His arms did not swing at his sides, but hung loosely.

A third-person narrative uses the pronoun *he*, *she*, or *they*. This voice allows the writer to have some distance from the characters.

Now answer these questions (you'll find answers on page 218):

What is the effect of the third person voice on the description?

_____

_____

_____

Is the description emotional or objective?

_____

_____

_____

Where is the metaphor, and what is the purpose of it?

_____

_____

_____

Would the same effect have been possible if the passage were written in first person?

_____

_____

_____

Third person narration allows the writer to maintain a distance from the characters. Sometimes this allows the writer to judge, or cast a critical eye on the proceedings. Sometimes the writer remains objective. See what the interaction is between the writer and the character. In prose analysis, you may be asked to identify what the effect of a certain word or description has on the character. You may need to identify what the author's intent is, if he or she is objective or subjective in tone.

Most fiction writers use the past tense, although the action of the story can take place in the past, present, or future.

TENSE

We've talked about character and voice. Be aware that novels can take place in the future, present, or past. Past tense is the most popular tense. Most stories are told after all the events have transpired. Frequently, events will be *foreshadowed*. Foreshadowing is when the author hints at something that is going to happen later. Some modern novels are written in present tense. Very few novels are written in future tense. Even if it's a novel about the future, it is usually told from the perspective of a narrator who has already lived through the events.

A foreshadowed event is an event that the author suggests will happen later.

PLOT

It seems strange to talk about plots so far into a discussion of fiction, but as you may know already, plots are dependent on all the things you've learned. Plots are the stories. These are the things that happen to the characters. Plots, when they are at their best, reveal things to the reader about the characters. It is always better to show something about a character through a storyline rather than to just tell the reader.

A plot is the story.

SHORT STORIES

Short stories differ from novels in that they cannot, due to their form, go into the character and narrative development that novels can. They tend to show something small but important. Because they are so short, they tend to be more focused. Let's look at the opening of the short story "Harrison Bergeron" from Kurt Vonnegut's collection of short stories entitled *Welcome to the Monkey House:*

> The year was 2081, and everybody was finally equal. They weren't only equal before God and the law. They were equal every which way. Nobody was smarter than anybody else. Nobody was better looking than anybody else. Nobody was stronger or quicker than anybody else. All this equality was due to the 211th, 212th, and 213th Amendments to the Constitution, and to the unceasing vigilance of agents of the United States Handicapper General.
>
> Some things about living still weren't quite right, though. April, for instance, still drove people crazy by not being springtime. And it was in that clammy month that the H-G men took George and Hazel Bergeron's fourteen-year-old son, Harrison, away.

Now answer these questions (answers are on page 218):

What is the effect of the two opening paragraphs?

_____

_____

_____

Is the narrator subjective or objective?

_____

_____

_____

Who do you suspect the protagonist is going to be?

_____

_____

_____

Short stories do not have the same character and narrative development that novels do. Short stories tend to be more focused.

NONFICTION PROSE

Prose writing that is not made up is called nonfiction. The essay, biography, and autobiography are the most familiar forms of nonfiction prose. Keep in mind that novels may have elements that are autobiographical or biographical, but if facts are made up around the autobiographical element, the work is still considered fiction.

The most familiar forms of nonfiction prose are the essay, the biography, and the autobiography.

Let's analyze a selection from the autobiography of Maya Angelou, *I Know Why the Caged Bird Sings:*

> My name had lost its ring of familiarity and I had to be nudged to go and receive my diploma. All my preparations had fled. I neither marched up to the stage like a conquering Amazon, nor did I look in the audience for Bailey's nod of approval. Marguerite Johnson, I heard the name again, my honors were read, there were noises in the audience of appreciation, and I took my place on the stage as rehearsed.
> I thought about colors I hated: ecru, puce, lavender, beige, and black.

Try these questions (the answer key is on page 218):

What is the tone used by the speaker?

_____

_____

_____

What similes does Angelou use?

_____

_____

_____

What is the overall effect on the reader?

_____

_____

_____

You'll notice that the devices of nonfiction may be similar to the devices of fiction and poetry. Maya Angelou, an accomplished poet, uses poetic language in her autobiography. It helps to define who she is. Analyzing nonfiction is similar to fiction. Who are the characters? What is the tone?

If you are reading essays, decide what the author's point of view is. Is he or she *dispassionate, ironic, satirical, didactic (instructive)*? If the author is presenting a thesis, is she for, against, or neutral? Sometimes nonfiction is objective, sometimes it is subjective. Decide this while you read. You can go back and reread specific lines referred to in a question after reading the essay as a whole.

| For an essay, determine the author's point of view.

Let's analyze part of a speech by the great jurist Learned Hand, entitled "The Spirit of Liberty":

> What is this spirit of liberty? I cannot define it; I can only tell you my own faith. The spirit of liberty is the spirit which is not too sure that it is right; the spirit of liberty is the spirit which seeks to understand the minds of other men and women; the spirit of liberty is the spirit which weighs their interests alongside its own without bias; the spirit of liberty remembers that not even a sparrow falls to earth unheeded; the spirit of liberty is the spirit of Him who, near two thousand years ago, taught mankind a lesson it has never learned, but has never quite forgotten: that there may be a kingdom where the least shall be heard and considered side by side with the greatest.

What is the allusion Hand makes in his speech?
Why does he use that particular allusion?

_____

_____

_____

What is the personification? Does it enhance the
essay?

_____

_____

_____

What is the overall tone?

_____

_____

_____

To whom might a speech like this be addressed?

_____

_____

_____

You can check your answers on page 218.

So, as you can see again, many of the same criteria you used in analyzing
fiction will work with nonfiction as well.

ANALYZING PROSE DRILL

Let's try a multiple-choice drill similar to what you'll see on the Literature Test. The passage is from Henry James's *Washington Square.*

"Try and make a clever woman of her, Lavinia; I should like her to be a clever woman."

Mrs. Penniman, at this, looked thoughtful a moment. "My dear Austin," she then inquired, "do
(5) you think it is better to be clever than to be good?"

"Good for what?" asked the Doctor. "You are good for nothing unless you are clever."

From this assertion Mrs. Penniman saw no reason to dissent; she possibly reflected that her
(10) own great use in the world was owing to her aptitude for many things.

"Of course I wish Catherine to be good," the Doctor said next day; "but she won't be any the less virtuous for not being a fool. I am not afraid
(15) of her being wicked; she will never have the salt of malice in her character. She is 'as good as good bread,' as the French say; but six years hence I don't want to have to compare her to good bread-and-butter."

(20) "Are you afraid she will be insipid? My dear brother, it is I who supply the butter; so you needn't fear!" said Mrs. Penniman, who had taken in hand the child's "accomplishments," overlooking her at the piano, where Catherine displayed a
(25) certain talent, and going with her to the dancing-class, where it must be confessed that she made but a modest figure.

Mrs. Penniman was a tall, thin, fair, rather faded woman, with a perfectly amiable disposition, a high
(30) standard of gentility, a taste for light literature, and a certain foolish indirectness and obliquity of character. She was romantic; she was sentimental; she had a passion for little secrets and mysteries—a very innocent passion, for her secrets had hitherto
(35) always been as unpractical as addled eggs.

1. The word "overlooking" (line 23) is meant to suggest that Mrs. Penniman does which of the following?

   (A) ignores Catherine's talent
   (B) teaches Catherine how to play the piano
   (C) supervises Catherine's piano playing
   (D) discourages Catherine
   (E) hires Catherine's tutors

2. Which of the following does Mrs. Penniman use metaphorically to talk about her influence on Catherine?

   (A) addled eggs
   (B) butter
   (C) bread
   (D) salt
   (E) a fool

3. What does the author imply by the term "it must be confessed that she made but a modest figure?" (lines 26-27)

   (A) Catherine was trim and fit.
   (B) Catherine was unaware of her talent.
   (C) Catherine was unlikely to brag.
   (D) Catherine was a talented dancer.
   (E) Catherine was just an average dancer.

4. The narrative tone in the above piece can best be described as

   (A) melodramatic
   (B) ironic
   (C) sardonic
   (D) didactic
   (E) observant

5. The narrative point of view in the above passage is that of a

   (A) third person
   (B) protagonist
   (C) second person
   (D) sarcastic first person
   (E) detached first person

Check your answers on page 218.

14

Analyzing Drama

Drama is a form of literature unlike any other. It is intended to be acted out. As such, you are always a little cheated, a little bit removed from the author's vision of the work, when you read a play quietly to yourself.

The elements of the play are not so different from the elements of any good story. There must be compelling characters, a good plot, and an underlying theme. A good play always *shows* what is inherent in people. A really great play reveals something true about the society it depicts.

Because plays are written to be acted out, they seem to be slightly more connected to the audience than other forms of literature. There is an inseparable bond between a play and the culture and times in which it was written. Some plays, such as Shakespeare's *Henry* plays, reveal history in a tragic way. In a time when a majority of people could not read, plays brought literature and art to the masses.

When analyzing a play, ask yourself the same questions you have asked in the previous sections. If literary devices, such as metaphors, are used, what is the effect? What is the tone of a character? Is the character an archetype, designed to represent something more than what he appears to be? In a play, the characters are central to explicating the plot—there is no narrative to move it along. Some playwrights have used the device of a "narrator" to get around this problem. In *Our Town*, Thornton Wilder's play, the stage manager wanders on and off stage commenting on the action, giving the audience his own personal insight.

Look at a passage from *Pygmalion* by George Bernard Shaw:

ELIZA: (Overwhelmed) Ah-ah-ow-oo!

HIGGINS: There! That's all you'll get out of Eliza. Ah-ah-ow-oo! No use explaining. As a military man you ought to know that. Give her orders: that's what she wants. Eliza: you are to live here for the next six months, learning how to speak beautifully, like a lady in a florist's shop. If you're good and do whatever you're told, you shall sleep in a proper bedroom, and have lots to eat, and money to buy chocolates and take rides in taxis. If you're naughty and idle, you will sleep in the back kitchen among the black beetles, and be walloped by Mrs. Pearce with a broomstick. At the end of six months you shall go to Buckingham Palace in a carriage, beautifully dressed. If the King finds out you're not a lady, you will be taken to the Tower of London, where your head will be cut off as a warning to other presumptuous flower girls. If you are not found out, you shall have a present of seven and six pence to start life with as a lady in a shop. If you refuse this offer you will be a most ungrateful and wicked girl, and the angels will weep for you.

What does the dialogue show you about the two characters?

_____

_____

_____

What metaphor does Higgins use?

_____

_____

_____

Where does Higgins use personification?

_____

_____

_____

How do you feel about the characters after reading the exchange between them?

_____

_____

_____

Answers are on page 219.

Let's try a multiple-choice drill on a passage from Henrik Ibsen's *An Enemy of the People*.

PETER STOCKMANN: To my mind the whole thing only seems to mean that you are seeking another outlet for your combativeness. You want to pick a quarrel with your superiors—an old habit of

(5) yours. You cannot put up with any authority over you. You look askance at anyone who occupies a superior official position; you regard him as a personal enemy, and then any stick is good enough to beat him with. But now I have called your

(10) attention to the fact that the town's interests are at stake—and, incidentally, my own too. And therefore I must tell you, Thomas, that you will find me inexorable with regard to what I am about to require you to do.

(15) DR. STOCKMANN: And what is this?

PETER STOCKMANN: As you have been so indiscreet as to speak of this delicate matter to outsiders, despite the fact that you ought to have treated it as entirely official and confidential, it is

(20) obviously impossible to hush it up now. All sorts of rumors will get about directly, and everybody who has a grudge against us will take care to embellish these rumors. So, it will be necessary for you to refute them publicly.

(25) DR. STOCKMANN: I! How? I don't understand.

PETER STOCKMANN: What we shall expect is that, after making further investigations, you will come to the conclusion that the matter is not by any means as dangerous or as critical as you

(30) imagined in the first instance.

DR. STOCKMAN: Oho!—so that is what you expect!

1. One can infer from the dialogue between Peter Stockmann and Dr. Stockmann that their relationship is

   (A) friendly
   (B) adversarial
   (C) conspiratorial
   (D) familial
   (E) neutral

2. Which of the following is metaphor used by Peter Stockmann when speaking to Dr. Stockmann?

   (A) "put up with any authority over you" (lines 5-6)
   (B) "any stick is good enough to beat him with" (lines 8-9)
   (C) "the town's interests are at stake" (lines 10-11)
   (D) "so indiscreet as to speak of this delicate matter" (lines 16-17)
   (E) "rumors will get about directly" (line 21)

3. In context, the word "directly" (line 21) most closely means which of the following?

   (A) "in a straightforward manner"
   (B) "constantly"
   (C) "to many different people"
   (D) "maliciously"
   (E) "soon"

4. The tone of the last line is best described as

   (A) sarcastic
   (B) enthusiastic
   (C) didactic
   (D) melodramatic
   (E) mysterious

5. The tone of the line, "As you have been so indiscreet as to speak of this delicate matter to outsiders" (lines 16-18), can best be described as

   (A) ambiguous
   (B) benevolent
   (C) amused
   (D) disdainful
   (E) understanding

You can check your answers on page 219.

As you can see, drama is as complex a literary form as poetry or prose. While most drama is written as prose, early classic dramas were written in verse. If you're analyzing a drama that is written in verse, use the same techniques that you use to analyze poetry.

Some drama is written in prose and some drama is written in poetry.

15

The Final Word on the Literature Test

THE FINAL WORD BEFORE THE DIAGNOSTIC

Don't forget about your pacing. Accuracy is more important than speed.

You've already covered quite a lot of information in going through the ways to analyze poetry, prose, and drama. Review the opening section on cracking the test again. After taking the diagnostic, review your performance and ask yourself where your study time could be best spent. Don't waste a lot of time on one or two little things that you've missed. Review the pacing chart before your exam. Keep track of your goals. Often, you don't need to get that many more questions correct to get a really great score.

Don't forget:

- Put the passages in order before you begin. Which do you want to do first and which do you want to do last?

- Take a minute to read the passage.

- Tackle the specific/line reference questions first. Read a few lines before and after.

- Answer the general questions last.

AFTER THE DIAGNOSTIC, ASK YOURSELF:

Did you run out of time?

Don't forget to skip around. Do the easy questions first; then go back to the hard ones.

If you ran out of time and didn't get to a few easy questions at the end of the test, you're not discriminating enough when it comes to skipping questions. Don't linger in any one place too long—one question is *never* worth five minutes of your time.

Keep in mind:

> 60 MINUTES for 60 QUESTIONS =
> ONE QUESTION PER MINUTE

Did you get a lot of "easy" questions wrong?

Sometimes, when you look back and review, you can't believe you got such an easy question wrong. Slow down. Did you read the question correctly the first time around? Did you pick the right answer but circle an incorrect choice? Rushing is the major cause of avoidable errors.

Don't rush. This only results in careless errors.

Did you mismark answers on your answer sheet?

It's not at all uncommon to skip a question and then fill in all the subsequent answers one up on your answer sheet. It's a really good idea to fill in answers in blocks: in other words, work on one passage in your booklet, then transfer the eight or nine answers to the answer sheet all at once. Then go back to your booklet and work on the next passage.

Always circle the answer you choose and cross out answers you decide are wrong. If you want to go back later and recheck a particular answer, you will avoid doubling your work. Let's say, for example, you decided that the answer to question 6 was either (A) or (D). If you come back to it later, you won't waste time considering (B), (C), and (E) if you've already crossed them out.

Are you skipping around while taking the test?

Be a discriminating test taker! Look for a passage or poem that appeals to you and begin with that. If you by any chance see a passage that you recognize, you'll be a few steps ahead of the game—do that one first.

FINALLY, GOOD LUCK! YOU'RE WELL PREPARED!

Make sure to show up at the test site with lots of #2 pencils (with good erasers), a reliable watch, and a small snack to munch in case you have to wait or if you're taking more than one test in a day. Remember, test results take six weeks to arrive, so when you're finished, go home, refuse to talk about it, and wait with supreme confidence for well-deserved scores.

Try bubbling in your answers a page at a time instead of a question at a time.

Remember, you don't have to do the passages or questions in the order presented.

PART ◆ VI

Answer Key to Drills

Literary Terms

Drill #1, page 180

1. S
2. P
3. S
4. M
5. A
6. P
7. M
8. S
9. M
10. A

Drill #2, page 181

1. AN
2. O
3. OX
4. A
5. OX
6. AN
7. O
8. A
9. OX
10. O

Drill #3, page 182

1. P
2. A
3. F
4. S

"A Pilgrim's Solace," pages 186-187

Analogy—his heart and the day
Personification—He refers to his joy as something that could die.
Alliteration—Stay, sweet, shines
Personification—joy perishing
Main idea—I know it's morning, but I wish you didn't have to take off.

Hughes poem, page 187

Alliteration—steam, smoke, slime
Personification—Two dollars buys shoes
Alliteration again—buys for the baby; bright bowl of brass is beautiful
Allusion—Kings David and Solomon
Metaphor—bowl like cymbals
The techniques give a clear image of his life. The **rhythm** has the effect of mimicking the actions he describes.

Dickinson poem, page 188

Similes:—frigate like a book; coursers like a page
Metaphors:—This traverse … without … toll … the chariot that bears a human soul
The **effect** is to convey a simple idea (that of a book carrying you away) with vivid imagery.
Main idea—You can get "carried away" through books and reading.

Pope poem, pages 189-190

Personification—representing death as a person
Alliteration—let me languish into life; Sister Spirit; Steals my senses, shuts my sight
Personification—representing the grave as having no victory
The **meter** quickens as the poem progresses. The **effect** is to mimic the quickening movement as the soul goes to heaven at the end.
Punctuation—The question marks and exclamation points underscore the dramatic subject.
Naturally, the elements complement the subject.
Classic poem—regular rhythm, classic theme (death), classic form, with regular rhyme scheme

"Madman's Song," pages 191-192

1. C
2. D
3. B
4. A
5. C

Analyzing Prose

Moby-Dick analysis,
pages 195-196

First-person narrative makes the story more personal and also gives you just one perspective.
Metaphor—November in my soul.
Effect—bringing to life a vivid image
Narrator—insightful and interesting, but rather unhappy character
Third person would have made the story less personal, less in the mind of the main character.

Of Mice and Men analysis,
page 197

Third person has the effect of making it a more objective description. This third person, you may notice, is simply describing the action that takes place, not really getting into the minds of the characters.
The **description** is very objective.
Metaphor—"the way a bear drags his paws." The effect of the metaphor is to evoke an image of the character.
If it were in the **first person**, the passage would not have been so objective; we would be seeing the action from the perspective of one or the other character.

**"Harrison Bergeron" analysis,
page 199**

The **effect** of the first two paragraphs is that they set up the story—the history in general, and the specific characters you will be introduced to.
The narrator is **subjective**; he is passing judgment on the characters and the situation. Harrison Bergeron is the protagonist.

I Know Why the Caged Bird Sings analysis, page 200

The **tone** is mildly critical of the situation.
Simile—"like a conquering Amazon"
The **overall effect** is sympathy.
The reader is meant to understand the plight of the young girl through her subjective description of the day.

**Learned Hand speech analysis,
page 201**

The **allusion** is to Christ ("Him who, near two thousand years ago"). He alludes to a message that most are familiar with.
Personification here is referring to the spirit of liberty.
He describes liberty as if it were a person. It makes the image clear.
The **tone** is passionate and subjective. He has a strong point of view and intends to impart it.
The **speech** might be addressed to politicians, or a church group.

**Analyzing Prose Drill,
pages 202-203**

1. C
2. B
3. E
4. E
5. A

Analyzing Drama

Pygmalion **analysis, page 207**

The **dialogue** here immediately sets up the difference in education and class between the two characters. It also sets up the story.

Metaphor—like a lady in a florist's shop

Personification—the angels will weep for you

You feel **sympathy** more for Eliza than for Higgins. He is set up as an unsympathetic character.

An Enemy of the People,
pages 208-209

1. B
2. B
3. E
4. A
5. D

PART VII

The Princeton Review
SAT II: Literature Tests

SAT II: LITERATURE TEST

SECTION 1

Your responses to the Literature Test questions should be filled in on Section One of your answer sheet.

LITERATURE TEST

<u>Directions</u>: This test consists of selections from literary works and questions on their content, form, and style. After reading each passage or poem, choose the best answer to each question and fill in the corresponding oval on the answer sheet.

<u>Note</u>: **Pay particular attention to the requirement of questions that contain the words NOT, LEAST, or EXCEPT.**

<u>Questions 1–10.</u> Read the following passage carefully before you choose your answers.

Ripe Figs

Maman-Nainaine said that when the figs were ripe Babette might go to visit her cousins down on the Bayou-Lafourche where the sugar cane grows. Not that the ripening of figs had the
(5) least thing to do with it, but that is the way Maman-Nainaine was.

It seemed to Babette a very long time to wait; for the leaves upon the trees were tender yet, and the figs were like little hard green
(10) marbles.

But warm rains came along and plenty of strong sunshine, and though Maman-Nainaine was as patient as the statue of la Madone, and Babette as restless as a hummingbird, the first
(15) thing they both knew it was hot summertime. Every day Babette danced out to where the fig-trees were in a long line against the fence. She walked slowly beneath them, carefully peering between the gnarled, spreading branches. But
(20) each time she came disconsolate away again. What she saw there finally was something that made her sing and dance the whole long day.

When Maman-Nainaine sat down in her stately way to breakfast the following morning,
(25) her muslin cap standing like an aureole about her white, placid face, Babette approached. She bore a dainty porcelain platter, which she set down before her godmother. It contained a dozen purple figs, fringed around with their
(30) rich green leaves.

"Ah," said Maman-Nainaine arching her eyebrows, "how early the figs have ripened this year!"

"Oh," said Babette. "I think they have
(35) ripened very late."

"Babette," continued Maman-Nainaine, as she peeled the very plumpest figs with her pointed silver fruit-knife, "you will carry my love to them all down on Bayou-Lafourche. And tell
(40) your Tante Frosine I shall look for her at Toussaint—when the chrysanthemums are in bloom."

1. In the passage, the ripening figs are symbolic of

(A) the fruits of labor
(B) the maturation of Babette
(C) the difficulty of life
(D) the enigma of nature
(E) the battle between Maman-Nainaine and Babette

2. The phrase "but that is the way Maman-Nainaine was" suggests which of the following about Maman-Nainaine?

(A) She was not aware of the seriousness of the situation.
(B) She was an overly strict woman.
(C) Her actions had their own logic.
(D) She doled out punishments for no reason.
(E) Figs were her favorite fruit.

3. What is the effect of the disagreement (lines 1-8)?

(A) It illustrates Maman-Nainaine's bad judgment.
(B) It serves to illustrate the patience of Maman-Nainaine and the impatience of Babette.
(C) It demonstrates a passage of time.
(D) It makes Babette appear spoiled and insolent.
(E) It shows how argumentative Babette can be.

GO ON TO THE NEXT PAGE

4. The word "aureole" (line 25) is probably meant to suggest which of the following?

   (A) A halo
   (B) Maman-Nainaine's cap
   (C) A frame around her face
   (D) A bright light
   (E) A warning to Babette

5. In the passage, Maman-Nainaine's attitude toward Babette can best be characterized as

   (A) contemptuous
   (B) flippant
   (C) reluctantly accepting
   (D) joyously optimistic
   (E) wisely patient

6. All of the following pairs of words illustrate the difference between Maman-Nainaine and Babette EXCEPT:

   (A) "patient" (line 13) and "restless" (line 14)
   (B) "early" (line 32) and "late" (line 35)
   (C) "green" (line 9) and "purple" (line 29)
   (D) "sat" (line 23) and "danced" (line 16)
   (E) "ripe" (line 2) and "bloom" (line 42)

7. What is the effect of the last line of the passage?

   (A) It shows that Maman-Nainaine is clearly illogical.
   (B) It serves as ironic counterpoint to the rest of the story.
   (C) It advances the symbolism introduced with the ripening figs.
   (D) It introduces a literary allusion.
   (E) It advances the story beyond its scope.

8. Maman-Nainaine's peeling of "the very plumpest figs" (line 37) illustrates which of the following about her?

   (A) She is making Babette wait just a bit longer.
   (B) She is a skilled cook.
   (C) She is superstitious.
   (D) She is a refined woman.
   (E) She enjoys teasing Babette.

9. The word "though" (line 12) implies which of the following in the context of the sentence?

   (A) The two women were in disagreement.
   (B) Patience is a virtue when waiting for something.
   (C) Figs were not really important.
   (D) Their patience and impatience had no effect on nature.
   (E) Maman-Nainaine's patience was annoying to Babette.

10. The narrative point of view of the passage as a whole is that of

   (A) an amused impartial observer
   (B) a first-person impartial observer
   (C) the protagonist
   (D) an unreliable narrator
   (E) a third-person objective observer

GO ON TO THE NEXT PAGE →

Questions 11–19. Read the following poem carefully before you choose your answers.

On His Deceased Wife

Methought I saw my late espoused Saint
    Brought to me like Alcestis from the grave,
    Whom Jove's great son to her glad husband gave.
    Rescu'd from death by force though pale and faint.
(5) Mine as whom wash't from spot of childbed taint,
    Purification in the old law did save,
    And such, as yet once more I trust to have
    Full sight of her in Heaven without restraint,
Came vested all in white, pure as her mind:
(10) Her face was vail'd, yet to my fancied sight,
    Love, sweetness, goodness, in her person shin'd
So clear, as in no face with more delight.
    But O, as to embrace me she inclined
    I wak'd, she fled, and day brought back my night.

11. "Whom Jove's great son" (line 3) acts as which of the following?

    (A) A play on words
    (B) A contradiction
    (C) Hyperbole
    (D) Mythological allusion
    (E) Allegory

12. Line 4 refers to which of the following?

    I. "my late espoused Saint" (line 1)
   II. "Alcestis" (line 2)
  III. "her glad husband" (line 3)

    (A) I only
    (B) II only
    (C) I and II only
    (D) II and III only
    (E) I and III only

13. In context, the word "save" (line 6) means which of the following?

    (A) preserve
    (B) keep in health
    (C) deliver from sin and punishment
    (D) rescue from harm
    (E) maintain

14. The change of the length of the last line is meant to suggest

    (A) a contrast between dreaming and waking states
    (B) the poet's depression
    (C) an allusion to the sonnet form
    (D) a parallel to the opening quatrain
    (E) that the writer is optimistic about the future

15. In context, "my fancied sight" (line 10) suggests that the author is

    (A) imbuing his deceased wife with qualities she did not have
    (B) unable to separate reality from dreams
    (C) capriciously conjuring up his wife's image
    (D) dreaming
    (E) suffering from delusions

GO ON TO THE NEXT PAGE

16. The author's attitude toward his wife can best be described as

    (A) inconsolable
    (B) reverential
    (C) hopeful
    (D) incongruous
    (E) obsequious

17. The poem is primarily concerned with

    (A) the mourning process
    (B) the struggle against dying
    (C) the injustice of death
    (D) the nature of immortality
    (E) a belief in heaven

18. What is the effect of using the word "glad" (line 3) instead of "happy" or "joyous"?

    (A) It suggests that the husband is overwhelmed.
    (B) It links to "great" and "gave" by alliteration.
    (C) It stresses that the husband is a particular person.
    (D) It distinguishes between "Jove's great son" and the husband.
    (E) It alludes to "I" in line 1.

19. Which of the following are terms of opposition in the poem?

    (A) "embrace" and "inclined" (line 13)
    (B) "day" and "night" (line 14)
    (C) "full sight" and "without restraint" (line 8)
    (D) "wash't" (line 5) and "purification" (line 6)
    (E) "sight" (line 10) and "shined" (line 11)

GO ON TO THE NEXT PAGE

Questions 20–28. Read the following passage carefully before you choose your answers.

Keenly alive to this prejudice of hers, Mr. Keeble stopped after making his announcement, and had to rattle the keys in his pocket in order to acquire the necessary courage to continue.

(5) He was not looking at his wife, but he knew just how forbidding her expression must be. This task of his was no easy, congenial task for a pleasant summer morning.

"She says in her letter," proceeded Mr.

(10) Keeble, his eyes on the carpet and his cheeks a deeper pink, "that young Jackson has got the chance of buying a big farm . . . in Lincolnshire, I think she said . . . if he can raise three thousand pounds."

(15) He paused, and stole a glance at his wife. It was as he had feared. She had congealed. Like some spell, the name had apparently turned her to marble. It was like the Pygmalion and Galatea business working the wrong way round.

(20) She was presumably breathing, but there was no sign of it.

"So I was just thinking," said Mr. Keeble, producing another *obbligato* on the keys, "it just crossed my mind . . . it isn't as if the thing

(25) were speculation . . . the place is apparently coining money . . . present owner only selling because he wants to go abroad . . . it occurred to me . . . and they would pay good interest on the loan. . . ."

(30) "What loan?" enquired the statue icily, coming to life.

20. Which of the following is the intended effect of the pauses in Mr. Keeble's conversation?

(A) It demonstrates that he is a feeble man.
(B) It makes his speech disjointed.
(C) It shows his hesitancy in approaching his wife.
(D) It slows the rhythm of the conversation.
(E) It elucidates his main point.

21. Which of the following expresses an allusion made in the passage?

(A) "interest on the loan"(lines 28-29)
(B) "no sign of it"(lines 20-21)
(C) "turned her to marble"(lines 17-18)
(D) "in Lincolnshire"(lines 12-13)
(E) "the Pygmalion and Galatea business"(lines 18-19)

22. All of the following represent metaphors used by the author EXCEPT:

(A) "She had congealed"(line 16)
(B) "enquired the statue icily"(line 30)
(C) "coming to life"(line 31)
(D) "presumably breathing"(line 20)
(E) "like some spell"(lines 16-17)

23. The phrase "the place is apparently coining money" (lines 25-26) is meant to imply

(A) the farm is presently engaged in illegal activities
(B) the farm is profitable
(C) the investment is unnecessary
(D) the farm serves as a bank for the local people
(E) Lincolnshire is a profitable place to live

24. Which of the following expresses Mr. Keeble's wife's feeling toward the loan?

(A) Amused detachment
(B) Utter disgust
(C) Prejudicial opposition
(D) Blatant apathy
(E) Neutrality

GO ON TO THE NEXT PAGE

25. All of the following are physical manifestations of Mr. Keeble's anticipation of his wife's response EXCEPT:

    (A) "had to rattle the keys" (line 3)
    (B) "was not looking at his wife" (line 5)
    (C) "keenly alive" (line 1)
    (D) "producing another *obbligato*" (line 23)
    (E) "his eyes on the carpet" (line 10)

26. The phrase "in Lincolnshire, I think she said" implies that which of the following is true of Keeble?

    (A) Keeble is unaware of the location of the farm.
    (B) Keeble thinks the location is unimportant.
    (C) Keeble's memory is failing.
    (D) Keeble is attempting to appear casual.
    (E) Keeble wants to conceal the location from his wife.

27. Keeble's relationship with his wife is such that

    I. he needs her approval
    II. he is afraid of her
    III. he is intimidated by her

    (A) II only
    (B) III only
    (C) II and III only
    (D) I and III only
    (E) I, II, and III

28. The last line implies which of the following?

    (A) Mr. Keeble's wife is not interested in lending money.
    (B) Mr. Keeble's wife is interested in the proposition.
    (C) Mr. Keeble has succeeded in his mission.
    (D) Mr. Keeble's wife is keeping an open mind about the loan.
    (E) Mr. Keeble's wife wants to hear more about the loan.

GO ON TO THE NEXT PAGE

Questions 29-37. Read the following passage carefully before you choose your answers.

On the back rest of my lifeguard's chair is painted a cross—true, a red cross, signifying bandages, splints, spirits of ammonia, and sunburn unguents. Nevertheless, it comforts
(5) me. Each morning, as I mount into my chair, my athletic and youthfully fuzzy toes expertly gripping the slats that make a ladder, it is as if I am climbing into an immense, rigid, loosely fitting vestment.
(10) Again, in each of my roles I sit attentively perched on the edge of an immensity. That the sea, with its multiform and mysterious hosts, its savage and senseless rages, no longer comfortably serves as a divine metaphor
(15) indicates how severely humanism has corrupted the apples of our creed. We seek God now in flowers and good deeds, and the immensities of blue that surround the little scabs of land upon which we draw our lives to their unsatisfactory
(20) conclusions are suffused by science with vacuous horror. I myself can hardly bear the thought of stars, or begin to count the mortalities of coral. But from my chair the sea, slightly distended by my higher perspective,
(25) seems a misty old gentleman stretched at his ease in an immense armchair which has for arms the arms of this bay and for an antimacassar the freshly laundered sky. Sail boats float on his surface like idle and
(30) unrelated but benevolent thoughts. The soughing of the surf is the rhythmic lifting of his ripple stitched vest as he breathes. Consider. We enter the sea with a shock; our skin and blood shout in protest. But, that
(35) instant, that leap, past, what do we find? Ecstasy and buoyance. Swimming offers a parable. We struggle and thrash, and drown; we succumb, even in despair, and float, and are saved.

29. The narrative in the above piece is from the point of view of

(A) a first-person narrator
(B) an accomplished essayist presenting a thesis
(C) an omniscient observer
(D) an objective observer
(E) a critical third-person narrator

30. It can be inferred that the narrator views the ocean as

(A) something to be feared
(B) a metaphor for God
(C) an unrelenting force of nature
(D) a friend
(E) an enemy

31. Which of the following best describes the narrator's tone?

(A) Annoyed yet sympathetic
(B) Detached and disinterested
(C) Disgusted yet optimistic
(D) Hopeful yet frightened
(E) Moral and didactic

32. What can be inferred from the line "in each of my roles" (line 10)?

(A) The narrator works part-time as an actor.
(B) The narrator likes to imagine himself doing other things.
(C) The narrator has some other, possibly religious, work.
(D) The lifeguard job is multifaceted.
(E) The narrator is referring to his personal life.

33. The last line suggests that

(A) working hard is the best way to succeed
(B) the best way to salvation is to give in to a higher authority
(C) no matter how hard one works, one will die
(D) life is a contradiction
(E) the sea is cruel and uncaring

GO ON TO THE NEXT PAGE →

34. The word "Nevertheless" (line 4) suggests

    (A) the lifeguard finds religious comfort in a
        symbol that is not religious
    (B) the symbol is inherently threatening
    (C) most people would not understand what is
        meant by the symbol
    (D) the symbol is aesthetically pleasing
    (E) the symbol does not comfort other people

35. In describing the sea, the narrator uses which of the
    following techniques?

    I. Irony
    II. Metaphor
    III. Personification

    (A) I only
    (B) I and II only
    (C) II and III only
    (D) I and III only
    (E) I, II, and III

36. The tone of the line "we seek God now in flowers
    and good deeds" (lines 16-17) can best be described
    as

    (A) bitter
    (B) uplifting
    (C) amused
    (D) disappointed
    (E) disgusted

37. Each of the following serves as a religious symbol
    in the piece EXCEPT:

    (A) the chair
    (B) splints
    (C) the red cross
    (D) the sea
    (E) swimming

GO ON TO THE NEXT PAGE

<u>Questions 38–45.</u> Read the following poem carefully before you choose your answers.

Fable

In heaven
Some little blades of grass
Stood before God.
"What did you do?"
(5) Then all save one of the little blades
Began eagerly to relate
The merits of their lives.
This one stayed a small way behind,
Ashamed.
(10) Presently, God said,
"And what did *you* do?"
The little blade answered, "O my Lord,
Memory is bitter to me,
For if I did good deeds
(15) I know not of them."
Then God, in all his splendor,
Arose from his throne.
"O best little blade of grass!" he said.

—*Stephen Crane*

38. It can be inferred that the speaker(s) in line 4 is/are

(A) an angel
(B) St. Peter
(C) the blades of grass
(D) God
(E) the one little blade of grass

39. God's attitude toward the little blade of grass may best be described as

(A) condescending
(B) neutral
(C) admiring
(D) disdainful
(E) morally superior

40. The main idea of the poem is that

(A) it is better to do nothing than too much
(B) it is better to forget if you have done something wrong
(C) it is better to be modest than to be boastful
(D) it is better to keep your problems to yourself
(E) if you need to tell your bad deeds to someone, you are not worthy of respect

GO ON TO THE NEXT PAGE →

41. The word "presently" (line 10) means which of the following in the context of the poem?

    I. At this time
   II. In a little while
  III. At once

  (A) I only
  (B) II only
  (C) I and III only
  (D) II and III only
  (E) I, II, and III

42. It can be inferred that the small blade was "ashamed" (line 9) because

  (A) it was smaller that the others
  (B) it was disgusted with the other blades of grass
  (C) it didn't feel worthy of God's attention
  (D) it was bitter and lonely
  (E) it thought its acts greater than the others' acts

43. The fact that God called the one blade "O best" can best be characterized as

  (A) ironic
  (B) satiric
  (C) tragic
  (D) comic
  (E) unfortunate

44. What is the effect of lines 16–17 in relation to the rest of the poem?

  (A) They reveal God's egotism.
  (B) They heighten anticipation for the last line.
  (C) They shift the narrative voice.
  (D) They echo the last lines of the first stanza.
  (E) They reveal the poet's true feelings.

45. God's attitude toward the blades of grass as a group is

  (A) shameful
  (B) neutral
  (C) disgusted
  (D) disapproving
  (E) melancholy

GO ON TO THE NEXT PAGE

<u>Questions 46-54.</u> Read the following passage carefully before you choose your answers.

Everybody at all addicted to letter writing, without having much to say, which will include a large proportion of the female world at least, must feel with Lady Bertram, that she was out
(5) of luck in having such a capital piece of Mansfield news, as the certainty of the Grants going to Bath, occur at a time when she could make no advantage of it, and will admit that it must have been very mortifying to her to see it
(10) fall to the share of their thankless son, and treated as concisely as possible at the end of a long letter, instead of having it to spread over the largest part of a page of her own—For though Lady Bertram, rather at home in the
(15) epistolary line, having early in her marriage, from the want of other employment, and the circumstance of Sir Thomas's being in Parliament, got into the way of making and keeping correspondents, and formed for herself
(20) a very creditable, commonplace, amplifying style, so that a very little matter was enough for her; she could not do entirely without any; she must have something to write about, even to her niece, and being so soon to lose all the
(25) benefit of Dr. Grant's gouty symptoms and Mrs. Grant's morning calls, it was very hard upon her to be deprived of one of the last epistolary uses she could put them to.
There was a rich amends, however, preparing
(30) for her. Lady Bertram's hour of good luck came. Within a few days from the receipt of Edmund's letter, Fanny had one from her aunt, beginning thus:
"My dear Fanny,
(35) I take up my pen to communicate some very alarming intelligence, which I make no doubt will give you much concern."

46. The narrative tone in the above piece can be described as

(A) wry
(B) bitterly ironic
(C) detached
(D) melodramatic
(E) secretive

47. What is implied by the phrase "could make no advantage of it" (lines 7-8)?

(A) Lady Bertram could use the news to suit her best interest.
(B) Lady Bertram was unable to write about the news.
(C) Lady Bertram could not relay the news in a pleasant light.
(D) Lady Bertram could convey only part of the news.
(E) Lady Bertram was bound to secrecy.

48. In context, the word "want" (line 16) means

(A) requirement
(B) desire
(C) poverty
(D) lack
(E) defect

49. What is the "benefit" referred to in line 25?

(A) Friends with whom to visit
(B) The ability to assist others
(C) A house full of visitors
(D) People willing to write letters
(E) News to write about

50. The "amplifying style" (lines 20-21) is one in which

(A) things sound more important than they are
(B) small bits of news are stretched out to a long letter
(C) the speaker's voice is very loud
(D) people are made to sound grand
(E) one writes in a large, bold print

GO ON TO THE NEXT PAGE

51. It can be inferred that Sir Thomas is

    (A) Lady Bertram's son
    (B) Lady Bertram's husband
    (C) a boarder at Mansfield
    (D) a relative of the Grants
    (E) a friend of Lady Bertram

52. The last line serves to illustrate which of the following about Lady Bertram?

    (A) She has found something to write about.
    (B) She is spreading malicious rumors.
    (C) She is concerned about the news she is sending.
    (D) She is unaware of Fanny's feelings.
    (E) She is worried about her niece.

53. Lady Bertram is best described as

    (A) a social pariah
    (B) an unwanted family member
    (C) a disenfranchised member of society
    (D) a well-meaning aristocrat
    (E) a disillusioned elderly woman

54. The phrase "even to her niece" (lines 23-24) implies that Lady Bertram

    (A) doesn't much care for her niece
    (B) is unhappy with her niece
    (C) is uncomfortable around her niece
    (D) doesn't need to have much to say to her niece
    (E) dislikes the prospect of writing to her niece

GO ON TO THE NEXT PAGE

<u>Questions 55–60.</u> Read the following poem carefully before you choose your answers.

Blue Girls

Twirling your blue skirts, travelling the sward
Under the towers of your seminary,
Go listen to your teachers old and contrary
Without believing a word.

(5) Tie the white fillets then about your hair
And think no more of what will come to pass
Than bluebirds that go walking on the grass
And chattering on the air.

Practise your beauty, blue girls, before it fail;
(10) And I will cry with my loud lips and publish
Beauty which all our power shall never establish,
It is so frail.

For I could tell you a story which is true;
I know a woman with a terrible tongue,
(15) Blear eyes fallen from blue,
All her perfections tarnished—yet it is not long
Since she was lovelier than any of you.

—*John Crowe Ransom*

55. The tone of the poem can best be described as

    (A) romantic
    (B) mythic
    (C) sarcastic
    (D) optimistic
    (E) hopeful

56. The poem is primarily concerned with

    (A) the importance of beauty
    (B) the lesson to be learned from the past
    (C) the frivolity of spending too much time on
        vanity
    (D) telling a story for the girls' benefit
    (E) the permanence of death

57. "Blear eyes fallen from blue" (line 15) is most
    probably meant to suggest

    (A) that the woman's beauty has deteriorated
    (B) that the woman is tired
    (C) that the woman is going blind
    (D) that disease can happen suddenly
    (E) that the girls are responsible for the woman's
        loss of beauty

GO ON TO THE NEXT PAGE →

58. "And chattering on the air" (line 8) is probably meant to refer to

    I. the girls
    II. the bluebirds
    III. the teachers

    (A) I only
    (B) I and II only
    (C) I and III only
    (D) II and III only
    (E) I, II, and III

59. The author's characterization of the woman can best be described as

    (A) sympathetic yet disapproving
    (B) unyielding and hurtful
    (C) disdainful and disgusted
    (D) pleasant and nostalgic
    (E) warm and feeling

60. The phrases "without believing a word" (line 4) and "think no more" (line 6) illustrate the girls'

    (A) innate sense of suspicion
    (B) inherent difficulty understanding subjects
    (C) lack of concern about weighty subjects
    (D) frail nature
    (E) disregard for the feelings of others

S T O P

IF YOU FINISH BEFORE TIME IS CALLED, YOU MAY CHECK YOUR WORK ON THIS TEST ONLY.
DO NOT WORK ON ANY OTHER TEST IN THIS BOOK.

HOW TO SCORE THE PRINCETON REVIEW LITERATURE SUBJECT TEST

When you take the real exam, the proctors will collect your text booklet and bubble sheet and send your answer sheet to New Jersey where a computer (yes, a big, old-fashioned one that has been around since the '60s) looks at the pattern of filled-in ovals on your answer sheet and gives you a score. We couldn't include even a small computer with this book, so we are providing this more primitive way of scoring your exam.

DETERMINING YOUR SCORE

STEP 1 Using the answer key on the next page, determine how many questions you got right and how many you got wrong on the test. Remember, questions that you do not answer do not count as either right answers or wrong answers.

STEP 2 List the number of right answers here.

(A) _____

STEP 3 List the number of wrong answers here. Now divide that number by 4. (Use a calculator if you're feeling particularly lazy.)

(B) _____ ÷ 4 = (C) _____

STEP 4 Subtract the number of wrong answers divided by 4 from the number of correct answers. Round this score to the nearest whole number. This is your raw score.

(A) – (C) = _____

STEP 5 To determine your real score, take the number from Step 4 above and look it up in the left column of the Score Conversion Table on page 240; the corresponding score on the right is your score on the exam.

ANSWER KEY TO SAT II: LITERATURE DIAGNOSTIC TEST

1. B	16. B	31. E	46. A
2. C	17. A	32. C	47. B
3. B	18. B	33. B	48. D
4. A	19. B	34. A	49. E
5. E	20. C	35. C	50. B
6. E	21. E	36. D	51. B
7. C	22. D	37. B	52. A
8. A	23. B	38. D	53. D
9. D	24. C	39. C	54. D
10. E	25. C	40. C	55. A
11. D	26. D	41. B	56. C
12. C	27. D	42. C	57. A
13. C	28. A	43. A	58. B
14. A	29. A	44. B	59. A
15. D	30. B	45. B	60. C

SAT II LITERATURE TEST — SCORE CONVERSION TABLE

Recentered scale as of April 1995

Raw Score	College Board Scaled Score	Raw Score	College Board Scaled Score
60	800	25	510
59	800	24	500
58	800	23	500
57	790	22	490
56	780	21	480
55	770	20	470
54	760	19	460
53	750	18	450
52	740	17	450
51	730	16	440
50	720	15	430
49	710	14	420
48	700	13	410
47	690	12	400
46	690	11	400
45	680	10	390
44	670	09	380
43	660	08	370
42	650	07	360
41	650	06	350
40	640	05	350
39	630	04	340
38	620	03	330
37	610	02	320
36	600	01	310
35	600	00	300
34	590	−01	300
33	580	−02	290
32	570	−03	280
31	560	−04	270
30	550	−05	260
29	550	−06	250
28	540	−07	250
27	530	−08	240
26	520	−09 through −15	230

SAT II: LITERATURE TEST

SECTION 2

Your responses to the Literature Test questions should be filled in on Section Two of your answer sheet.

LITERATURE TEST

<u>Directions</u>: This test consists of selections from literary works and questions on their content, form, and style. After reading each passage or poem, choose the best answer to each question and fill in the corresponding oval on the answer sheet.

Note: Pay particular attention to the requirement of questions that contain the words NOT, LEAST, or EXCEPT.

<u>Questions 1-9</u>. Read the following poem carefully before you choose your answers.

Promises Like Pie-Crust

Promise me no promises,
   So will I not promise you:
Keep we both our liberties,
   Never false and never true:
(5) Let us hold the die uncast,
   Free to come as free to go:
For I cannot know your past,
   And of mine what can you know?

You, so warm, may once have been
(10) Warmer towards another one:
I, so cold, may once have seen
   Sunlight, once have felt the sun:
Who shall show us if it was
   Thus indeed in time of old?
(15) Fades the image from the glass,
   And the fortune is not told.

If you promised, you might grieve
   For lost liberty again:
If I promised, I believe
(20) I should fret to break the chain.
Let us be the friends we were,
   Nothing more but nothing less:
Many thrive on frugal fare
   Who would perish of excess.

1. The promises referred to in the poem are

  (A) pledges to share one another's innermost
      secrets
  (B) articles of incorporation
  (C) items in a prenuptial agreement
  (D) resolution never to see one another again
  (E) marriage vows

GO ON TO THE NEXT PAGE

2. In the second stanza, the speaker reveals that

   (A) she yearns for the love of someone who is oblivious of her
   (B) her listener has expressed more ardent sentiments toward her than she has expressed toward him
   (C) she does not reciprocate the feelings of her listener
   (D) she is incapable of deep emotional attachment
   (E) she is heartbroken over the end of a previous relationship

3. The speaker compares her current relationship with the person to whom the poem is addressed to

   (A) one between strangers
   (B) a roll of the dice
   (C) one governed by reciprocal obligations
   (D) a restrained diet of plain food
   (E) an image in a crystal ball

4. "Sunlight" (line 12) is used as a symbol for

   (A) innocence
   (B) genuine mutual love (of a previous relationship)
   (C) purity
   (D) absolute confidence in the rightness of a decision
   (E) perfect understanding

5. Which of the following is NOT implied in the poem as a reason to avoid entering into promises?

   (A) One person can never fully know another.
   (B) A promise can be broken without the person to whom the promise was made ever knowing.
   (C) To make a promise denies one of a degree of personal liberty.
   (D) One cannot be judged faithful or unfaithful to a commitment which has not been promised.
   (E) One can never fully know the situations or feelings of those who made successful and binding promises in the past.

6. In context, "fret" (line 20) most nearly means

   (A) irritate
   (B) chafe
   (C) agitate
   (D) worry
   (E) corrode

7. Which of the following best expresses the meaning of the last two lines of the poem?

   (A) Some people are not meant to enjoy the richness of life, just as some cannot digest rich food.
   (B) When it comes to relationships, something is better than nothing.
   (C) For some people, the potential of happiness is more satisfying than the reality of happiness, because the potential cannot be diminished over time.
   (D) Not every relationship is worth the risk entailed to the participants.
   (E) Relationships sometimes thrive between two people who meet only occasionally, which would not endure a more serious commitment.

8. The tone of the poem as a whole can best be described as

   (A) delicate but firm
   (B) disappointed but unapologetic
   (C) ambivalent but patronizing
   (D) world-weary and vague
   (E) harsh and unyielding

9. The simile of the title is apt because

   (A) both promises and pie-crust are sweet
   (B) both promises and pie-crust are meant to be filled
   (C) both promises and pie-crust are easily broken
   (D) the speaker has overindulged in rich food
   (E) the speaker denies herself all pleasures in life

GO ON TO THE NEXT PAGE

Questions 10-17. Read the following passage carefully before you choose your answers.

Studies serve for delight, for ornament, and for ability. Their chief use for delight is in privateness and retiring; for ornament, is in discourse; and for ability, is in the judgment and
(5) disposition of business. For expert men can execute, and perhaps judge of particulars, one by one; but the general counsels, and the plots and marshalling of affairs come best from those that are learned. To spend too much time in studies
(10) is sloth; to use them too much for ornament is affectation; to make judgment wholly by their rules is the humor of a scholar. They perfect nature, and are perfected by experience: for natural abilities are like natural plants, that need
(15) pruning by study; and studies themselves do give forth directions too much at large, except they be bounded in by experience. Crafty men contemn* studies, simple men admire them, and wise men use them; for they teach not their own
(20) use; but that is a wisdom without them and above them, won by observation. Read not to contradict and confute, nor to believe and take for granted, nor to find talk and discourse, but to weigh and consider.

*have contempt for

10. The author's primary purpose is to

(A) demonstrate a display of learned eloquence
(B) encourage pupils to study diligently
(C) discuss the proper use of learning
(D) distinguish the more serious from less dignified motives for study
(E) dissuade students from applying their learning to unethical pursuits

11. By "expert men" (line 5) the author most nearly means

(A) persons with competence in specific activities, but who lack general education
(B) persons who have mastered a craft or trade
(C) persons who carry out the decisions of others
(D) persons who have devoted themselves to their studies
(E) persons who conduct the concrete business of the day

12. The author compares "abilities" and "plants" (lines 14-15) in order to make the point that

(A) individuals must discipline themselves as they grow to maturity
(B) some students learn profusely while others learn little or slowly
(C) individuals must be nurtured and protected as growing plants must be
(D) education encourages individuals to develop in conformity with one another
(E) education shapes and refines an individual's innate qualities

13. Which of the following cautions is NOT conveyed in the passage?

(A) The organization of large undertakings is best left to persons who have read widely and deeply.
(B) It is possible to be overzealous in the pursuit of knowledge.
(C) One should not flaunt one's learning ostentatiously.
(D) Scholars should live in strict accordance with precepts gained through their study.
(E) The knowledge gained from books must be tested against one's firsthand experience in the world.

GO ON TO THE NEXT PAGE

14. With which of the following words or phrases could "admire" (line 18) be replaced without changing the meaning of the sentence?

    (A) are awed by
    (B) profess to respect
    (C) enjoy
    (D) are envious of
    (E) are naturally drawn toward

15. Which of these stylistic devices is most prominent in the author's prose?

    (A) Elaborate metaphor
    (B) Hyperbole
    (C) Neatly balanced syntactic oppositions
    (D) Alliteration
    (E) Long, convoluted sentences

16. Reading, according to the author, is above all else a source for one's

    (A) controversial opinions
    (B) moral and religious beliefs
    (C) quiet amusement
    (D) stimulating conversation
    (E) private deliberation

17. The tone of the passage can best be described as

    (A) pious
    (B) didactic
    (C) satiric
    (D) moralistic
    (E) contentious

GO ON TO THE NEXT PAGE

Questions 18-24. Read the following poem carefully before you choose your answers.

The Errand

"On you go now! Run, son, like the devil
And tell your mother to try
To find me a bubble for the spirit level
And a new knot for this tie."

(5) But still he was glad, I know, when I stood my ground,
Putting it up to him
With a smile that trumped his smile and his fool's errand,
Waiting for the next move in the game.

18. The theme of the poem concerns

(A) rites of passage which mark the beginning of adolescence
(B) the contest of wills between one generation and the next
(C) the futility of needless chores with which parents occupy their children
(D) a boy's developing relationship with his father as the boy matures
(E) the resentment that lingers in the poet's memory of childhood

19. The errand described in the poem is a quest for

(A) component parts that have no existence independent of the whole
(B) tools the speaker needs in order to continue his work
(C) someone in the neighborhood more foolish than the man's son
(D) degrees of understanding that come with maturity
(E) common ground on which father and son can identify with one another

20. Which of the following distinctions does NOT characterize the difference between the two stanzas?

(A) A shift from perfect rhyme to slant rhyme
(B) A change in speaker
(C) The passage of time—perhaps of many years
(D) A movement from metaphorical to literal language
(E) A switch from remembered speech to lyric meditation

21. Which of the following is implied by the poet's use of the word "still" (line 5)?

(A) The father's jovial spirits were not ultimately dampened when his son did not assume the errand.
(B) The father's pleased response to his son's refusal will continue indefinitely.
(C) The game between the father and son will continue indefinitely.
(D) The father did not express his gladness to his son.
(E) The boy's father was disappointed when his son did not assume the errand.

GO ON TO THE NEXT PAGE

22. Which of the following is nearest in meaning to "Putting it up to him" (line 6)?

    (A) demonstrating to him the poet's awareness of his joke
    (B) challenging him to find a bubble for himself
    (C) refusing defiantly to honor his request
    (D) handing up to him the items he had asked for
    (E) turning the joke back around on him

23. "Trumped" (line 7) is an allusion to

    (A) a dramatic fanfare announcing an arrival or significant development
    (B) a winning play in a game of cards
    (C) showy but worthless finery
    (D) a squashing sound under one's feet
    (E) the eclipse of one source of light by a brighter source

24. In the last line the poet suggests that

    (A) the father will send his son on another, more serious errand
    (B) the father's goal is to make his son appear ridiculous
    (C) the father's response to his son's recognition will be significantly delayed
    (D) the father will continue to good-humoredly tease and test his son
    (E) the father and son will always engage in prankish contests

GO ON TO THE NEXT PAGE

Questions 25-33. Read the following passage carefully before you choose your answers.

Joe's funeral was the finest thing Orange County had ever seen with Negro eyes. The motor hearse, the Cadillac and Buick carriages; Dr. Henderson there in his Lincoln; the hosts
(5) from far and wide. Then again the gold and red and purple, the gloat and glamor of the secret orders, each with its insinuations of power and glory undreamed of by the uninitiated. People on farm houses and mules;
(10) babies riding astride of brothers' and sisters' backs. The Elks band ranked at the church door and playing "Safe in the Arms of Jesus" with such a dominant drum rhythm that it could be stepped off smartly by the long line as it
(15) filed inside. The Little Emperor of the cross-roads was leaving Orange County as he had come—with the out-stretched hand of power.
Janie starched and ironed her face and came set in the funeral behind her veil. It was like a
(20) wall of stone and steel. The funeral was going on outside. All things concerning death and burial were said and done. Finish. End. Nevermore. Darkness. Deep hole. Dissolution. Eternity. Weeping and wailing
(25) outside. Inside the expensive black folds were resurrection and life. She did not reach outside for anything, nor did the things of death reach inside to disturb her calm. She sent her face to Joe's funeral, and herself went rollicking with
(30) the springtime across the world. After a while the people finished their celebration and Janie went on home.

25. Which of the following is the closest paraphrase of the first sentence of the passage?

(A) Joe's funeral was the finest display the black people of Orange County had ever seen.
(B) Joe's funeral was the finest display of black people that the white people of Orange County had ever seen.
(C) The finest looking black people in Orange County were all in evidence at Joe's funeral.
(D) The ceremony of Joe's funeral was not much compared to an average funeral for a white person in Orange County.
(E) Joe's funeral gave the white people in attendance a chance to experience the world from a black point of view.

26. The effect of the first paragraph is to

(A) contrast the pomp and display of the assembled mourners with Janie's genuine grief
(B) show how Joe's funeral was not in keeping with the tendencies of his life
(C) demonstrate the importance with which Joe was viewed in his community
(D) illustrate the fruitless nature of our attempts to disguise the starkness of death.
(E) emphasize the ephemerality of life

27. It can be surmised that the mourners at Joe's funeral

(A) are deeply grieved by Joe's death
(B) are exaggerating their respect for Joe out of sympathy for Janie
(C) are insincerely using Joe's funeral as an excuse for a flamboyant celebration
(D) are all members of a single, tight-knit community
(E) would be surprised to learn of Janie's sense of detachment from the proceedings

28. "Secret orders" (line 7) most probably refers to

(A) the self-importance felt by those driving expensive automobiles to the funeral
(B) the silent commands governing the conduct of some attendees at the funeral
(C) members of fraternal organizations who came to the funeral dressed in their clubs' regalia
(D) the haughty behavior of people attending the funeral whom the other attendees had never met or seen
(E) the majestic, heavenly hosts of which Joe is now presumably a member

GO ON TO THE NEXT PAGE →

29. Why is Janie's veil described as "a wall of stone and steel" (lines 19-20)?

    (A) The veil allows Janie to suppress her anguish and maintain her composure during the funeral.
    (B) The veil screens Janie from the accusing stares of the mourners at the funeral.
    (C) The veil represents the solidity of Janie's emotional state.
    (D) The veil allows Janie to endure the formal pretense of mourning at Joe's funeral, which is not in keeping with her true feelings.
    (E) The veil allows Janie to hide her true feelings from herself until after the funeral.

30. What is the effect of the phrase "the people finished their celebration" (line 31)?

    (A) It draws attention to the funeral's emphasis on the virtues of Joe's life and achievements.
    (B) It emphasizes the communal nature of the funeral, which brings together individuals from all ranks of society.
    (C) It emphasizes Janie's isolation from the others at the funeral.
    (D) It emphasizes the distances from which people had traveled to attend the funeral.
    (E) It points out that celebrations are by nature temporary, and must give way to the routines of daily life.

31. The style of the passage is characterized by the repeated use of

    (A) Black American dialect
    (B) grammatically incomplete sentences
    (C) religious imagery
    (D) ironic turns of phrase
    (E) oxymoron

32. Which of the following phrases from the passage best expresses Janie's emotional state during the funeral?

    (A) "gloat and glamor"
    (B) "starched and ironed"
    (C) "Darkness. Deep hole."
    (D) "Weeping and wailing"
    (E) "resurrection and life"

33. Which of the following inferences can be made about Janie's relationship to Joe?

    (A) Janie knew Joe only as a casual acquaintance and is unmoved by his death.
    (B) Janie cared deeply for Joe and has not yet fully experienced the shock of his death.
    (C) Janie felt a strong dislike for Joe and must disguise her antipathy at his funeral.
    (D) Janie's relationship with Joe was such that she feels unburdened and revitalized by his death.
    (E) Janie's feelings for Joe were a secret to the community and must be suppressed at his funeral.

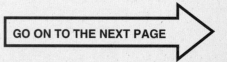

GO ON TO THE NEXT PAGE

Questions 34-42. Read the following poem carefully before you choose your answers.

The Mower to the Glowworms

Ye living lamps, by whose dear light
The nightingale does sit so late,
And studying all the summer night,
Her matchless songs does meditate;

(5) Ye country comets, that portend
No war nor prince's funeral,
Shining unto no higher end
Than to presage the grass's fall;

Ye glowworms, whose officious flame
(10) To wandering mowers shows the way,
That in the night have lost their aim,
And after foolish fires do stray;

Your courteous lights in vain you waste,
Since Juliana here is come,
(15) For she my mind hath so displaced
That I shall never find my home.

34. The speaker of the poem first addresses the glowworms by epithets that draw attention to the insects' natural

   (A) intelligence
   (B) tranquility
   (C) luminosity
   (D) inconsequence
   (E) mortality

35. The speaker of the poem describes glowworms as providing assistance to

   I. nightingales
   II. princes
   III. mowers

   (A) I only
   (B) II only
   (C) III only
   (D) I and III only
   (E) I, II, and III

36. In its context, the word "portend" (line 5)

   (A) means "predict," and alludes to the superstition that the motion of glowworms could be interpreted to foretell future events
   (B) means "predict," and alludes to the superstition that comets, meteors, and other natural phenomena were omens of evil
   (C) means "forecast," and alludes to the fact that the behavior of insects can be used to predict the next day's weather
   (D) means "imitate," and suggests that glowworms mimic the cyclical flight of comets
   (E) means "weigh," and makes clear that glowworms are oblivious to the dramatic upheavals of human life

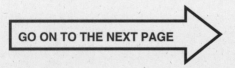

GO ON TO THE NEXT PAGE

37. Which of the following best expresses the meaning of "higher end" (line 7)?

    (A) Brighter level
    (B) Greater distance off the ground
    (C) Further boundary
    (D) Secret intention
    (E) Nobler purpose

38. Which of the following is the closest synonym for "officious," as it is used in line 9?

    (A) Helpful
    (B) Dim
    (C) Wandering
    (D) Bureaucratic
    (E) Meddlesome

39. The speaker implies that, without the glowworms, mowers who have "lost their aim" would be likely to

    (A) mow the wrong fields
    (B) conduct themselves disgracefully
    (C) fall in love
    (D) be distracted by other, mysterious sources of light
    (E) never find their way home

40. Which of the following is the best paraphrase for the last line of the poem?

    (A) I am blinded by my resentment toward her.
    (B) I will continue wandering forever.
    (C) I will never be myself again.
    (D) I will never go home without her.
    (E) I will never go to heaven.

41. The main verb of the sentence that constitutes the poem is

    (A) "sit" (line 2)
    (B) "waste" (line 13)
    (C) "come" (line 14)
    (D) "displaced" (line 15)
    (E) "find" (line 16)

42. "The Mower to the Glowworms" could most reasonably be considered

    (A) a celebration of fireflies
    (B) an elaborate compliment to a woman
    (C) an analysis of love at first sight
    (D) an allegory about the Holy Spirit
    (E) a commentary on the foolishness of mowers

GO ON TO THE NEXT PAGE

<u>Questions 43-53</u>. Read the following passage carefully before you choose your answers.

Rose: Times have changed since you was playing baseball, Troy. That was before the war. Times have changed a lot since then.

Troy: How in hell they done changed?

(5) Rose: They got lots of colored boys playing ball now. Baseball and football.

Bono: You right about that, Rose. Times have changed, Troy. You just come along too early.

(10) Troy: There ought not never have been no time called too early! Now you take that fellow . . . what's that fellow they had playing right field for the Yankees back then? You know who I'm talking about,

(15) Bono. Used to play right field for the Yankees.

Rose: Selkirk?

Troy: Selkirk! That's it! Man batting .269, understand? .269. What kind of sense that

(20) make? I was hitting .432 with thirty-seven home runs! Man batting .269 and playing right field for the Yankees! I saw Josh Gibson's* daughter yesterday. She walking around with raggedy shoes on her feet.

(25) Now I bet you Selkirk's daughter ain't walking around with raggedy shoes on her feet! I bet you that!

Rose: They got a lot of colored baseball players now. Jackie Robinson was the first. Folks

(30) had to wait for Jackie Robinson.

Troy: I done seen a hundred niggers play baseball better than Jackie Robinson. Hell, I know some teams Jackie Robinson couldn't even make! Jackie Robinson wasn't nobody.

(35) I'm talking about if you could play ball then they ought to have let you play. Don't care what color you were. Come telling me I come along too early. If you could play . . . then they ought to have let you play.

(40) *(Troy takes a long drink from the bottle.)*

Rose: You gonna drink yourself to death. You don't need to be drinking like that.

Troy: Death ain't nothing. I done seen him. Done wrastled with him. You can't tell me nothing

(45) about death. Death ain't nothing but a fastball on the outside corner. And you know what I'll do to that! Lookee here, Bono . . . am I lying? You get one of them fastballs, about waist height, over the outside corner of

(50) the plate where you can get the meat of the bat on it . . . and good god! You can kiss it goodbye. Now, am I lying?

Bono: Naw, you telling the truth there. I seen you do it.

(55) Troy: If I'm lying . . . that 450 feet worth of lying! *(Pause.)* That's all death is to me. A fastball on the outside corner.

Rose: I don't know why you want to get on talking about death.

(60) Troy: Ain't nothing wrong with talking about death. That's part of life. Everybody gonna die. You gonna die, I'm gonna die. Bono's gonna die. Hell, we all gonna die.

*Josh Gibson was a notable baseball player in the Negro Leagues.

43. It can be inferred that Troy played baseball

(A) before the outbreak of World War I
(B) long before the period in which Selkirk played right field for the Yankees
(C) before Jackie Robinson was born
(D) before the major leagues were racially integrated
(E) until his near brush with death

44. Which of the following best expresses the meaning of Troy's statement that "There ought not never have been no time called too early!" (lines 10-11)?

(A) We should judge past conditions in light of their historical context.
(B) It is a shame that we must wait for society's flaws to be corrected by progress and social change.
(C) Most individuals are born before the time period in which they could most prosper or succeed.
(D) The language we use to describe the world affects the way we experience the world.
(E) Despite the appearance of progress, social conditions do not really improve.

GO ON TO THE NEXT PAGE

45. Troy mentions his encounter with Josh Gibson's daughter in order to

    (A) prove that Selkirk had been unqualified to play right field for the Yankees
    (B) cite an example of a black athlete whose skills in his view exceeded those of Jackie Robinson
    (C) pay tribute to the greatest of right fielders in the Negro Leagues
    (D) illustrate the disparity in the economic rewards available to white and to black professional baseball players before the integration of major-league baseball
    (E) emphasize his point that times have not changed

46. Troy's tone in lamenting the injustice of his baseball career is one of

    (A) evenhanded objectivity
    (B) harsh political fervor
    (C) lingering resentment
    (D) naïve idealism
    (E) pompous self-pity

47. It can be inferred that Rose's feelings for Troy are characterized by

    (A) affectionate concern
    (B) sarcastic mockery
    (C) reverent admiration
    (D) apathetic dismissal
    (E) jealous anxiety

48. Troy begins a speech by personifying death, then proceeds to

    (A) ignore Rose's well-meaning advice
    (B) revert to his previous bragging about his prowess as a baseball player
    (C) elaborate a simile expressing his fearlessness of death
    (D) make an analogy that shows that he believes he can evade death
    (E) explain what he believes it will feel like to die

49. Troy's attitude toward death is primarily one of

    (A) contemptuous denial
    (B) naïve self-delusion
    (C) boastful nonchalance
    (D) awed anticipation
    (E) thinly-veiled cowardice

50. From the passage, it can be inferred that Troy and Bono are

    (A) opponents in a long-standing dispute
    (B) former teammates of Josh Gibson
    (C) baseball players of two different generations
    (D) flirtatious colleagues
    (E) old friends

51. The most appropriate setting for this dialogue would be

    (A) a school playground
    (B) a batting cage
    (C) Troy's front porch
    (D) a dinner party hosted by Bono
    (E) an office shared by the three characters

GO ON TO THE NEXT PAGE

52. Which of the following stylistic devices are employed by the playwright to evoke the atmosphere of the scene?

    I. Soliloquy
    II. Double entendre
    III. Nonstandard English

    (A) I only
    (B) II only
    (C) III only
    (D) I and III only
    (E) II and III only

53. Which of the following would most logically precede the discussion excerpted in this passage?

    (A) A discussion about whether Troy's son can expect to be discriminated against in his sports career because he is black
    (B) A debate over whether Troy should compete for a spot at the Yankees' spring training camp
    (C) A debate over the merits of racially integrated neighborhoods
    (D) A discussion of the great moments in Troy's baseball career
    (E) A discussion of persistent racial unrest in American society

Questions 54-60. Read the following passage carefully before you choose your answers.

The guest waked from a dream, and remembering his day's pleasure hurried to dress himself that it might sooner begin. He was sure from the way the shy little girl looked
(5) once or twice yesterday that she had at least seen the white heron, and now she must really be persuaded to tell. Here she comes now, paler than ever, and her worn old frock is torn and tattered, and smeared with pine pitch. The
(10) grandmother and the sportsman stand in the door together and question her, and the splendid moment has come to speak of the dead hemlock-tree by the green marsh.
    But Sylvia does not speak after all, though
(15) the old grandmother fretfully rebukes her, and the young man's kind appealing eyes are looking straight in her own. He can make them rich with money; he has promised it, and they are poor now. He is so well worth making
(20) happy, and he waits to hear the story she can tell.
    No, she must keep silence! What is it that suddenly forbids her and makes her dumb? Has she been nine years growing, and now, when
(25) the great world for the first time puts out a hand to her, must she thrust it aside for a bird's sake? The murmur of the pine's green branches in her ears, she remembers how the white heron came flying through the golden air and how
(30) they watched the sea and the morning together, and Sylvia cannot speak; she cannot tell the heron's secret and give its life away.

54. It can be inferred that the guest's anticipated "day's pleasure" centered around

    (A) his furthering his acquaintance with Sylvia
    (B) his hearing the end of a tale which Sylvia has promised to finish for him
    (C) his opportunity to make a carving from a petrified hemlock tree
    (D) his opportunity to photograph a white heron in its natural habitat
    (E) his opportunity to shoot a white heron

GO ON TO THE NEXT PAGE →

55. Which of the following is NOT an effect of the switch from past-tense narration to present-tense narration in the first paragraph?

    (A) It conveys the young man's surprise at the little girl's appearance.
    (B) It emphasizes the young man's suspense in waiting for her to speak.
    (C) It serves to heighten the reader's anticipation of the little girl's revelation.
    (D) It signals the narrator's switch from the guest's point of view to the little girl's.
    (E) It intensifies the reader's sense that this is a moment that both the young man and Sylvia have been eagerly awaiting.

56. Which of the following is the strongest enticement for Sylvia to lead the young man to where she has seen the white heron?

    (A) Her grandmother's failing health
    (B) Her respect for the young man's good intentions toward the heron
    (C) Her fear that the young man might take her away from her familiar surroundings
    (D) His promise of financial reward
    (E) Her loyalty to all the wild creatures of the region

57. Which of the following best articulates Sylvia's feelings toward the young man?

    (A) She hopes to win his esteem at any cost.
    (B) She is torn between her desire to please him and her contrary impulse not to assist him.
    (C) She is indifferent to his aims and toward him as a person.
    (D) She is repulsed by him personally, although she supports his endeavor.
    (E) She despises his mercenary motives.

58. Sylvia's own surprise at her reluctance to speak is best conveyed by

    (A) the narrator's emphasis on her and her grandmother's poverty
    (B) the narrator's admission that Sylvia had never before had the chance to fulfill someone's hopes as she might have fulfilled the young man's
    (C) the short sentences used to convey the choppiness of Sylvia's thoughts
    (D) Sylvia's memory of the pine tree and the view of the sea
    (E) the author's use of rhetorical questions to express Sylvia's own self-questioning

59. Sylvia is described in the passage as

    (A) achieving a new awareness and sense of herself
    (B) failing to honor a promise she had made to her grandmother
    (C) frustrating any hope she might have had of better getting to know the young man
    (D) persistently dismissive of other people's feelings
    (E) remaining faithful to her long-standing beliefs

60. Which of the following phrases from the passage is most nearly the antithesis of what the white heron represents to Sylvia?

    (A) "torn and tattered" (lines 8-9)
    (B) "splendid moment" (line 12)
    (C) "nine years growing" (line 18)
    (D) "the great world" (line 25)
    (E) "the golden air" (line 29)

S T O P

IF YOU FINISH BEFORE TIME IS CALLED, YOU MAY CHECK YOUR WORK ON THIS TEST ONLY.
DO NOT WORK ON ANY OTHER TEST IN THIS BOOK.

HOW TO SCORE THE PRINCETON REVIEW LITERATURE SUBJECT TEST

When you take the real exam, the proctors will collect your text booklet and bubble sheet and send your answer sheet to New Jersey where a computer (yes, a big, old-fashioned one that has been around since the '60s) looks at the pattern of filled-in ovals on your answer sheet and gives you a score. We couldn't include even a small computer with this book, so we are providing this more primitive way of scoring your exam.

DETERMINING YOUR SCORE

STEP 1   Using the answer key on the next page, determine how many questions you got right and how many you got wrong on the test. Remember, questions that you do not answer do not count as either right answers or wrong answers.

STEP 2   List the number of right answers here.

(A) _____

STEP 3   List the number of wrong answers here. Now divide that number by 4. (Use a calculator if you're feeling particularly lazy.)

(B) _____ ÷ 4 = (C) _____

STEP 4   Subtract the number of wrong answers divided by 4 from the number of correct answers. Round this score to the nearest whole number. This is your raw score.

(A) – (C) = _____

STEP 5   To determine your real score, take the number from Step 4 above and look it up in the left column of the Score Conversion Table on page 258; the corresponding score on the right is your score on the exam.

ANSWER KEY TO SAT II: LITERATURE DIAGNOSTIC TEST

1. E	16. E	31. B	46. C
2. B	17. B	32. E	47. A
3. D	18. D	33. D	48. C
4. B	19. A	34. C	49. C
5. B	20. D	35. D	50. E
6. B	21. A	36. B	51. C
7. E	22. A	37. E	52. C
8. A	23. B	38. A	53. A
9. C	24. D	39. D	54. E
10. C	25. A	40. C	55. B
11. A	26. C	41. B	56. D
12. E	27. E	42. B	57. B
13. D	28. C	43. D	58. E
14. A	29. D	44. B	59. A
15. C	30. C	45. D	60. D

SAT II LITERATURE TEST—SCORE CONVERSION TABLE

Recentered scale as of April 1995

Raw Score	College Board Scaled Score	Raw Score	College Board Scaled Score
60	800	25	510
59	800	24	500
58	800	23	500
57	790	22	490
56	780	21	480
55	770	20	470
54	760	19	460
53	750	18	450
52	740	17	450
51	730	16	440
50	720	15	430
49	710	14	420
48	700	13	410
47	690	12	400
46	690	11	400
45	680	10	390
44	670	09	380
43	660	08	370
42	650	07	360
41	650	06	350
40	640	05	350
39	630	04	340
38	620	03	330
37	610	02	320
36	600	01	310
35	600	00	300
34	590	−01	300
33	580	−02	290
32	570	−03	280
31	560	−04	270
30	550	−05	260
29	550	−06	250
28	540	−07	250
27	530	−08	240
26	520	−09 through −15	230

ABOUT THE AUTHOR

Liz Buffa joined The Princeton Review in 1989. She has taught classes in test prep for the SAT I, LSAT, GMAT, and SAT II: English Subject Tests. She is a graduate of Wellesley College. She lives in Locust Valley, New York, with her husband and two sons, David and Paul.

The Princeton Review
Diagnostic Test Form ○ Side 1

1.

YOUR NAME: _____
(Print)   Last   First   M.I.

SIGNATURE: _____ DATE: ___/___/___

HOME ADDRESS: _____
(Print)   Number and Street

_____
City   State   Zip Code

PHONE NO.: _____
(Print)

IMPORTANT: Please fill in these boxes exactly as shown on the back cover of your test book.

5. YOUR NAME

First 4 letters of last name				FIRST INIT	MID INIT

2. TEST FORM

3. TEST CODE

4. REGISTRATION NUMBER

6. DATE OF BIRTH

MONTH	DAY		YEAR	
JAN				
FEB				
MAR				
APR				
MAY				
JUN				
JUL				
AUG				
SEP				
OCT				
NOV				
DEC				

7. SEX
- MALE
- FEMALE

SCANTRON® FORM NO. F-592-KIN
© SCANTRON CORPORATION 1989 3289-C553-5
ALL RIGHTS RESERVED.

Begin with number 1 for each new section of the test. Leave blank any extra answer spaces.

SECTION 1

1 Ⓐ Ⓑ Ⓒ Ⓓ Ⓔ 26 Ⓐ Ⓑ Ⓒ Ⓓ Ⓔ 51 Ⓐ Ⓑ Ⓒ Ⓓ Ⓔ 76 Ⓐ Ⓑ Ⓒ Ⓓ Ⓔ
2 Ⓐ Ⓑ Ⓒ Ⓓ Ⓔ 27 Ⓐ Ⓑ Ⓒ Ⓓ Ⓔ 52 Ⓐ Ⓑ Ⓒ Ⓓ Ⓔ 77 Ⓐ Ⓑ Ⓒ Ⓓ Ⓔ
3 Ⓐ Ⓑ Ⓒ Ⓓ Ⓔ 28 Ⓐ Ⓑ Ⓒ Ⓓ Ⓔ 53 Ⓐ Ⓑ Ⓒ Ⓓ Ⓔ 78 Ⓐ Ⓑ Ⓒ Ⓓ Ⓔ
4 Ⓐ Ⓑ Ⓒ Ⓓ Ⓔ 29 Ⓐ Ⓑ Ⓒ Ⓓ Ⓔ 54 Ⓐ Ⓑ Ⓒ Ⓓ Ⓔ 79 Ⓐ Ⓑ Ⓒ Ⓓ Ⓔ
5 Ⓐ Ⓑ Ⓒ Ⓓ Ⓔ 30 Ⓐ Ⓑ Ⓒ Ⓓ Ⓔ 55 Ⓐ Ⓑ Ⓒ Ⓓ Ⓔ 80 Ⓐ Ⓑ Ⓒ Ⓓ Ⓔ
6 Ⓐ Ⓑ Ⓒ Ⓓ Ⓔ 31 Ⓐ Ⓑ Ⓒ Ⓓ Ⓔ 56 Ⓐ Ⓑ Ⓒ Ⓓ Ⓔ 81 Ⓐ Ⓑ Ⓒ Ⓓ Ⓔ
7 Ⓐ Ⓑ Ⓒ Ⓓ Ⓔ 32 Ⓐ Ⓑ Ⓒ Ⓓ Ⓔ 57 Ⓐ Ⓑ Ⓒ Ⓓ Ⓔ 82 Ⓐ Ⓑ Ⓒ Ⓓ Ⓔ
8 Ⓐ Ⓑ Ⓒ Ⓓ Ⓔ 33 Ⓐ Ⓑ Ⓒ Ⓓ Ⓔ 58 Ⓐ Ⓑ Ⓒ Ⓓ Ⓔ 83 Ⓐ Ⓑ Ⓒ Ⓓ Ⓔ
9 Ⓐ Ⓑ Ⓒ Ⓓ Ⓔ 34 Ⓐ Ⓑ Ⓒ Ⓓ Ⓔ 59 Ⓐ Ⓑ Ⓒ Ⓓ Ⓔ 84 Ⓐ Ⓑ Ⓒ Ⓓ Ⓔ
10 Ⓐ Ⓑ Ⓒ Ⓓ Ⓔ 35 Ⓐ Ⓑ Ⓒ Ⓓ Ⓔ 60 Ⓐ Ⓑ Ⓒ Ⓓ Ⓔ 85 Ⓐ Ⓑ Ⓒ Ⓓ Ⓔ
11 Ⓐ Ⓑ Ⓒ Ⓓ Ⓔ 36 Ⓐ Ⓑ Ⓒ Ⓓ Ⓔ 61 Ⓐ Ⓑ Ⓒ Ⓓ Ⓔ 86 Ⓐ Ⓑ Ⓒ Ⓓ Ⓔ
12 Ⓐ Ⓑ Ⓒ Ⓓ Ⓔ 37 Ⓐ Ⓑ Ⓒ Ⓓ Ⓔ 62 Ⓐ Ⓑ Ⓒ Ⓓ Ⓔ 87 Ⓐ Ⓑ Ⓒ Ⓓ Ⓔ
13 Ⓐ Ⓑ Ⓒ Ⓓ Ⓔ 38 Ⓐ Ⓑ Ⓒ Ⓓ Ⓔ 63 Ⓐ Ⓑ Ⓒ Ⓓ Ⓔ 88 Ⓐ Ⓑ Ⓒ Ⓓ Ⓔ
14 Ⓐ Ⓑ Ⓒ Ⓓ Ⓔ 39 Ⓐ Ⓑ Ⓒ Ⓓ Ⓔ 64 Ⓐ Ⓑ Ⓒ Ⓓ Ⓔ 89 Ⓐ Ⓑ Ⓒ Ⓓ Ⓔ
15 Ⓐ Ⓑ Ⓒ Ⓓ Ⓔ 40 Ⓐ Ⓑ Ⓒ Ⓓ Ⓔ 65 Ⓐ Ⓑ Ⓒ Ⓓ Ⓔ 90 Ⓐ Ⓑ Ⓒ Ⓓ Ⓔ
16 Ⓐ Ⓑ Ⓒ Ⓓ Ⓔ 41 Ⓐ Ⓑ Ⓒ Ⓓ Ⓔ 66 Ⓐ Ⓑ Ⓒ Ⓓ Ⓔ 91 Ⓐ Ⓑ Ⓒ Ⓓ Ⓔ
17 Ⓐ Ⓑ Ⓒ Ⓓ Ⓔ 42 Ⓐ Ⓑ Ⓒ Ⓓ Ⓔ 67 Ⓐ Ⓑ Ⓒ Ⓓ Ⓔ 92 Ⓐ Ⓑ Ⓒ Ⓓ Ⓔ
18 Ⓐ Ⓑ Ⓒ Ⓓ Ⓔ 43 Ⓐ Ⓑ Ⓒ Ⓓ Ⓔ 68 Ⓐ Ⓑ Ⓒ Ⓓ Ⓔ 93 Ⓐ Ⓑ Ⓒ Ⓓ Ⓔ
19 Ⓐ Ⓑ Ⓒ Ⓓ Ⓔ 44 Ⓐ Ⓑ Ⓒ Ⓓ Ⓔ 69 Ⓐ Ⓑ Ⓒ Ⓓ Ⓔ 94 Ⓐ Ⓑ Ⓒ Ⓓ Ⓔ
20 Ⓐ Ⓑ Ⓒ Ⓓ Ⓔ 45 Ⓐ Ⓑ Ⓒ Ⓓ Ⓔ 70 Ⓐ Ⓑ Ⓒ Ⓓ Ⓔ 95 Ⓐ Ⓑ Ⓒ Ⓓ Ⓔ
21 Ⓐ Ⓑ Ⓒ Ⓓ Ⓔ 46 Ⓐ Ⓑ Ⓒ Ⓓ Ⓔ 71 Ⓐ Ⓑ Ⓒ Ⓓ Ⓔ 96 Ⓐ Ⓑ Ⓒ Ⓓ Ⓔ
22 Ⓐ Ⓑ Ⓒ Ⓓ Ⓔ 47 Ⓐ Ⓑ Ⓒ Ⓓ Ⓔ 72 Ⓐ Ⓑ Ⓒ Ⓓ Ⓔ 97 Ⓐ Ⓑ Ⓒ Ⓓ Ⓔ
23 Ⓐ Ⓑ Ⓒ Ⓓ Ⓔ 48 Ⓐ Ⓑ Ⓒ Ⓓ Ⓔ 73 Ⓐ Ⓑ Ⓒ Ⓓ Ⓔ 98 Ⓐ Ⓑ Ⓒ Ⓓ Ⓔ
24 Ⓐ Ⓑ Ⓒ Ⓓ Ⓔ 49 Ⓐ Ⓑ Ⓒ Ⓓ Ⓔ 74 Ⓐ Ⓑ Ⓒ Ⓓ Ⓔ 99 Ⓐ Ⓑ Ⓒ Ⓓ Ⓔ
25 Ⓐ Ⓑ Ⓒ Ⓓ Ⓔ 50 Ⓐ Ⓑ Ⓒ Ⓓ Ⓔ 75 Ⓐ Ⓑ Ⓒ Ⓓ Ⓔ 100 Ⓐ Ⓑ Ⓒ Ⓓ Ⓔ

The Princeton Review
Diagnostic Test Form ○ Side 2

Completely darken bubbles with a No. 2 pencil. If you make a mistake, be sure to erase mark completely. Erase all stray marks.

Begin with number 1 for each new section of the test. Leave blank any extra answer spaces.

SECTION 2

1	A	B	C	D	E	26	A	B	C	D	E	51	A	B	C	D	E	76	A	B	C	D	E
2	A	B	C	D	E	27	A	B	C	D	E	52	A	B	C	D	E	77	A	B	C	D	E
3	A	B	C	D	E	28	A	B	C	D	E	53	A	B	C	D	E	78	A	B	C	D	E
4	A	B	C	D	E	29	A	B	C	D	E	54	A	B	C	D	E	79	A	B	C	D	E
5	A	B	C	D	E	30	A	B	C	D	E	55	A	B	C	D	E	80	A	B	C	D	E
6	A	B	C	D	E	31	A	B	C	D	E	56	A	B	C	D	E	81	A	B	C	D	E
7	A	B	C	D	E	32	A	B	C	D	E	57	A	B	C	D	E	82	A	B	C	D	E
8	A	B	C	D	E	33	A	B	C	D	E	58	A	B	C	D	E	83	A	B	C	D	E
9	A	B	C	D	E	34	A	B	C	D	E	59	A	B	C	D	E	84	A	B	C	D	E
10	A	B	C	D	E	35	A	B	C	D	E	60	A	B	C	D	E	85	A	B	C	D	E
11	A	B	C	D	E	36	A	B	C	D	E	61	A	B	C	D	E	86	A	B	C	D	E
12	A	B	C	D	E	37	A	B	C	D	E	62	A	B	C	D	E	87	A	B	C	D	E
13	A	B	C	D	E	38	A	B	C	D	E	63	A	B	C	D	E	88	A	B	C	D	E
14	A	B	C	D	E	39	A	B	C	D	E	64	A	B	C	D	E	89	A	B	C	D	E
15	A	B	C	D	E	40	A	B	C	D	E	65	A	B	C	D	E	90	A	B	C	D	E
16	A	B	C	D	E	41	A	B	C	D	E	66	A	B	C	D	E	91	A	B	C	D	E
17	A	B	C	D	E	42	A	B	C	D	E	67	A	B	C	D	E	92	A	B	C	D	E
18	A	B	C	D	E	43	A	B	C	D	E	68	A	B	C	D	E	93	A	B	C	D	E
19	A	B	C	D	E	44	A	B	C	D	E	69	A	B	C	D	E	94	A	B	C	D	E
20	A	B	C	D	E	45	A	B	C	D	E	70	A	B	C	D	E	95	A	B	C	D	E
21	A	B	C	D	E	46	A	B	C	D	E	71	A	B	C	D	E	96	A	B	C	D	E
22	A	B	C	D	E	47	A	B	C	D	E	72	A	B	C	D	E	97	A	B	C	D	E
23	A	B	C	D	E	48	A	B	C	D	E	73	A	B	C	D	E	98	A	B	C	D	E
24	A	B	C	D	E	49	A	B	C	D	E	74	A	B	C	D	E	99	A	B	C	D	E
25	A	B	C	D	E	50	A	B	C	D	E	75	A	B	C	D	E	100	A	B	C	D	E

SECTION 3

1	A	B	C	D	E	26	A	B	C	D	E	51	A	B	C	D	E	76	A	B	C	D	E
2	A	B	C	D	E	27	A	B	C	D	E	52	A	B	C	D	E	77	A	B	C	D	E
3	A	B	C	D	E	28	A	B	C	D	E	53	A	B	C	D	E	78	A	B	C	D	E
4	A	B	C	D	E	29	A	B	C	D	E	54	A	B	C	D	E	79	A	B	C	D	E
5	A	B	C	D	E	30	A	B	C	D	E	55	A	B	C	D	E	80	A	B	C	D	E
6	A	B	C	D	E	31	A	B	C	D	E	56	A	B	C	D	E	81	A	B	C	D	E
7	A	B	C	D	E	32	A	B	C	D	E	57	A	B	C	D	E	82	A	B	C	D	E
8	A	B	C	D	E	33	A	B	C	D	E	58	A	B	C	D	E	83	A	B	C	D	E
9	A	B	C	D	E	34	A	B	C	D	E	59	A	B	C	D	E	84	A	B	C	D	E
10	A	B	C	D	E	35	A	B	C	D	E	60	A	B	C	D	E	85	A	B	C	D	E
11	A	B	C	D	E	36	A	B	C	D	E	61	A	B	C	D	E	86	A	B	C	D	E
12	A	B	C	D	E	37	A	B	C	D	E	62	A	B	C	D	E	87	A	B	C	D	E
13	A	B	C	D	E	38	A	B	C	D	E	63	A	B	C	D	E	88	A	B	C	D	E
14	A	B	C	D	E	39	A	B	C	D	E	64	A	B	C	D	E	89	A	B	C	D	E
15	A	B	C	D	E	40	A	B	C	D	E	65	A	B	C	D	E	90	A	B	C	D	E
16	A	B	C	D	E	41	A	B	C	D	E	66	A	B	C	D	E	91	A	B	C	D	E
17	A	B	C	D	E	42	A	B	C	D	E	67	A	B	C	D	E	92	A	B	C	D	E
18	A	B	C	D	E	43	A	B	C	D	E	68	A	B	C	D	E	93	A	B	C	D	E
19	A	B	C	D	E	44	A	B	C	D	E	69	A	B	C	D	E	94	A	B	C	D	E
20	A	B	C	D	E	45	A	B	C	D	E	70	A	B	C	D	E	95	A	B	C	D	E
21	A	B	C	D	E	46	A	B	C	D	E	71	A	B	C	D	E	96	A	B	C	D	E
22	A	B	C	D	E	47	A	B	C	D	E	72	A	B	C	D	E	97	A	B	C	D	E
23	A	B	C	D	E	48	A	B	C	D	E	73	A	B	C	D	E	98	A	B	C	D	E
24	A	B	C	D	E	49	A	B	C	D	E	74	A	B	C	D	E	99	A	B	C	D	E
25	A	B	C	D	E	50	A	B	C	D	E	75	A	B	C	D	E	100	A	B	C	D	E

FOR TPR USE ONLY	V1	V2	V3	V4	M1	M2	M3	M4	M5	M6	M7	M8

The Princeton Review
Diagnostic Test Form ○ Side 1

1.

YOUR NAME: _____
(Print)   Last   First   M.I.

SIGNATURE: _____   DATE: ___ / ___ / ___

HOME ADDRESS: _____
(Print)   Number and Street

_____
City   State   Zip Code

PHONE NO.: _____
(Print)

IMPORTANT: Please fill in these boxes exactly as shown on the back cover of your test book.

2. TEST FORM

3. TEST CODE

4. REGISTRATION NUMBER

5. YOUR NAME

First 4 letters of last name | FIRST INIT | MID INIT

6. DATE OF BIRTH

MONTH	DAY	YEAR
JAN		
FEB		
MAR		
APR		
MAY		
JUN		
JUL		
AUG		
SEP		
OCT		
NOV		
DEC		

7. SEX
- MALE
- FEMALE

Begin with number 1 for each new section of the test. Leave blank any extra answer spaces.

SECTION 1

(Answer bubbles 1–100, each with options A B C D E)

The Princeton Review
Diagnostic Test Form ○ Side 2

Completely darken bubbles with a No. 2 pencil. If you make a mistake, be sure to erase mark completely. Erase all stray marks.

Begin with number 1 for each new section of the test. Leave blank any extra answer spaces.

SECTION 2

1	A	B	C	D	E	26	A	B	C	D	E	51	A	B	C	D	E	76	A	B	C	D	E
2	A	B	C	D	E	27	A	B	C	D	E	52	A	B	C	D	E	77	A	B	C	D	E
3	A	B	C	D	E	28	A	B	C	D	E	53	A	B	C	D	E	78	A	B	C	D	E
4	A	B	C	D	E	29	A	B	C	D	E	54	A	B	C	D	E	79	A	B	C	D	E
5	A	B	C	D	E	30	A	B	C	D	E	55	A	B	C	D	E	80	A	B	C	D	E
6	A	B	C	D	E	31	A	B	C	D	E	56	A	B	C	D	E	81	A	B	C	D	E
7	A	B	C	D	E	32	A	B	C	D	E	57	A	B	C	D	E	82	A	B	C	D	E
8	A	B	C	D	E	33	A	B	C	D	E	58	A	B	C	D	E	83	A	B	C	D	E
9	A	B	C	D	E	34	A	B	C	D	E	59	A	B	C	D	E	84	A	B	C	D	E
10	A	B	C	D	E	35	A	B	C	D	E	60	A	B	C	D	E	85	A	B	C	D	E
11	A	B	C	D	E	36	A	B	C	D	E	61	A	B	C	D	E	86	A	B	C	D	E
12	A	B	C	D	E	37	A	B	C	D	E	62	A	B	C	D	E	87	A	B	C	D	E
13	A	B	C	D	E	38	A	B	C	D	E	63	A	B	C	D	E	88	A	B	C	D	E
14	A	B	C	D	E	39	A	B	C	D	E	64	A	B	C	D	E	89	A	B	C	D	E
15	A	B	C	D	E	40	A	B	C	D	E	65	A	B	C	D	E	90	A	B	C	D	E
16	A	B	C	D	E	41	A	B	C	D	E	66	A	B	C	D	E	91	A	B	C	D	E
17	A	B	C	D	E	42	A	B	C	D	E	67	A	B	C	D	E	92	A	B	C	D	E
18	A	B	C	D	E	43	A	B	C	D	E	68	A	B	C	D	E	93	A	B	C	D	E
19	A	B	C	D	E	44	A	B	C	D	E	69	A	B	C	D	E	94	A	B	C	D	E
20	A	B	C	D	E	45	A	B	C	D	E	70	A	B	C	D	E	95	A	B	C	D	E
21	A	B	C	D	E	46	A	B	C	D	E	71	A	B	C	D	E	96	A	B	C	D	E
22	A	B	C	D	E	47	A	B	C	D	E	72	A	B	C	D	E	97	A	B	C	D	E
23	A	B	C	D	E	48	A	B	C	D	E	73	A	B	C	D	E	98	A	B	C	D	E
24	A	B	C	D	E	49	A	B	C	D	E	74	A	B	C	D	E	99	A	B	C	D	E
25	A	B	C	D	E	50	A	B	C	D	E	75	A	B	C	D	E	100	A	B	C	D	E

SECTION 3

1	A	B	C	D	E	26	A	B	C	D	E	51	A	B	C	D	E	76	A	B	C	D	E
2	A	B	C	D	E	27	A	B	C	D	E	52	A	B	C	D	E	77	A	B	C	D	E
3	A	B	C	D	E	28	A	B	C	D	E	53	A	B	C	D	E	78	A	B	C	D	E
4	A	B	C	D	E	29	A	B	C	D	E	54	A	B	C	D	E	79	A	B	C	D	E
5	A	B	C	D	E	30	A	B	C	D	E	55	A	B	C	D	E	80	A	B	C	D	E
6	A	B	C	D	E	31	A	B	C	D	E	56	A	B	C	D	E	81	A	B	C	D	E
7	A	B	C	D	E	32	A	B	C	D	E	57	A	B	C	D	E	82	A	B	C	D	E
8	A	B	C	D	E	33	A	B	C	D	E	58	A	B	C	D	E	83	A	B	C	D	E
9	A	B	C	D	E	34	A	B	C	D	E	59	A	B	C	D	E	84	A	B	C	D	E
10	A	B	C	D	E	35	A	B	C	D	E	60	A	B	C	D	E	85	A	B	C	D	E
11	A	B	C	D	E	36	A	B	C	D	E	61	A	B	C	D	E	86	A	B	C	D	E
12	A	B	C	D	E	37	A	B	C	D	E	62	A	B	C	D	E	87	A	B	C	D	E
13	A	B	C	D	E	38	A	B	C	D	E	63	A	B	C	D	E	88	A	B	C	D	E
14	A	B	C	D	E	39	A	B	C	D	E	64	A	B	C	D	E	89	A	B	C	D	E
15	A	B	C	D	E	40	A	B	C	D	E	65	A	B	C	D	E	90	A	B	C	D	E
16	A	B	C	D	E	41	A	B	C	D	E	66	A	B	C	D	E	91	A	B	C	D	E
17	A	B	C	D	E	42	A	B	C	D	E	67	A	B	C	D	E	92	A	B	C	D	E
18	A	B	C	D	E	43	A	B	C	D	E	68	A	B	C	D	E	93	A	B	C	D	E
19	A	B	C	D	E	44	A	B	C	D	E	69	A	B	C	D	E	94	A	B	C	D	E
20	A	B	C	D	E	45	A	B	C	D	E	70	A	B	C	D	E	95	A	B	C	D	E
21	A	B	C	D	E	46	A	B	C	D	E	71	A	B	C	D	E	96	A	B	C	D	E
22	A	B	C	D	E	47	A	B	C	D	E	72	A	B	C	D	E	97	A	B	C	D	E
23	A	B	C	D	E	48	A	B	C	D	E	73	A	B	C	D	E	98	A	B	C	D	E
24	A	B	C	D	E	49	A	B	C	D	E	74	A	B	C	D	E	99	A	B	C	D	E
25	A	B	C	D	E	50	A	B	C	D	E	75	A	B	C	D	E	100	A	B	C	D	E

FOR TPR USE ONLY	V1	V2	V3	V4	M1	M2	M3	M4	M5	M6	M7	M8

NOTES

NOTES

NOTES

NOTES

NOTES

NOTES

NOTES

NOTES

NOTES

NOTES

NOTES

Free!

Did you know that The Microsoft Network gives you one free month?

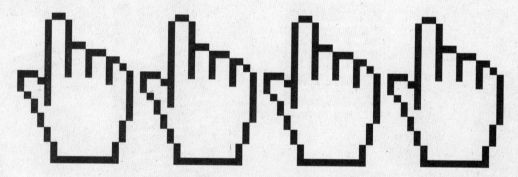

Call us at 1-800-FREE MSN. We'll send you a free CD to get you going.

Then, you can explore the World Wide Web for one month, free. Exchange e-mail with your family and friends. Play games, book airline tickets, handle finances, go car shopping, explore old hobbies and discover new ones. There's one big, useful online world out there. And for one month, it's a free world.

Call **1-800-FREE MSN,** Dept. 3197, for offer details or visit us at **www.msn.com**. Some restrictions apply.

The Microsoft Network

Microsoft® Where do you want to go today?®

FIND US...

International

Hong Kong
4/F Sun Hung Kai Centre
30 Harbour Road, Wan Chai,
Hong Kong
Tel: (011)85-2-517-3016

Japan
Fuji Building 40, 15-14
Sakuragaokacho, Shibuya Ku,
Tokyo 150, Japan
Tel: (011)81-3-3463-1343

Korea
Tae Young Bldg, 944-24,
Daechi- Dong, Kangnam-Ku
The Princeton Review- ANC
Seoul, Korea 135-280,
South Korea
Tel: (011)82-2-554-7763

Mexico City
PR Mex S De RL De Cv
Guanajuato 228 Col. Roma
06700 Mexico D.F., Mexico
Tel: 525-564-9468

Montreal
666 Sherbrooke St.
West, Suite 202
Montreal, QC H3A 1E7 Canada
Tel: (514) 499-0870

Pakistan
1 Bawa Park - 90 Upper Mall
Lahore, Pakistan
Tel: (011)92-42-571-2315

Spain
Pza. Castilla, 3 - 5° A, 28046
Madrid, Spain
Tel: (011)341-323-4212

Taiwan
155 Chung Hsiao East Road
Section 4 - 4th Floor,
Taipei R.O.C., Taiwan
Tel: (011)886-2-751-1243

Thailand
Building One, 99 Wireless Road
Bangkok, Thailand 10330
Tel: (662) 256-7080

Toronto
1240 Bay Street, Suite 300
Toronto M5R 2A7 Canada
Tel: (800) 495-7737
Tel: (716) 839-4391

Vancouver
4212 University Way NE,
Suite 204
Seattle, WA 98105
Tel: (206) 548-1100

National (U.S.)
We have over 60 offices around the U.S. and
run courses in over 400 sites. For courses and locations
within the U.S. call 1 (800) 2/Review and you will be
routed to the nearest office.